LESSONS I'VE LEARNED ALONG THE WAY

Daily Motivational Messages For Life's Unexpected Journey

LINCOLN BRYAN

Lessons I've Learned Along the Way

All Rights Reserved 2025

No part of this publication may be reproduced, distributed, or transmitted in any form or by any means, including photocopying, recording, or other electronic or mechanical methods, without the prior written permission of the author, except in the case of brief quotations embodied in critical reviews and certain other noncommercial uses permitted by copyright law.

©Copyright 2025 LINCOLN BRYAN

DEDICATION

To my beloved daughters, Brielle and Zariah,

As I reflect on the journey that has brought me to this moment, I am reminded of the two brightest lights in my life: you both. Your love, curiosity, and resilience inspire me daily to be a better person and leave a lasting legacy.

This book, Lessons I've Learned Along the Way, is a collection of wisdom, insights, and experiences I've gathered on my journey. As you read these pages, I hope you will glean wisdom, guidance, and encouragement to navigate your paths.

May these lessons inspire you to be brave, to take risks, and to pursue your dreams with passion and purpose. May you learn from my triumphs and mistakes and use them as stepping stones to create your unique journey.

I love you both more than words can express, and I am honored to share these lessons with you. May they bless you both now and in the coming years.

PREFACE

"Lessons I've Learned Along the Way" is a personal and introspective journey, born from the triumphs and tribulations of my own life. Reflecting on the twists and turns that have shaped me, I am reminded that growth and wisdom often emerge from the unexpected.

Within these pages, I invite you to join me on a path of self-discovery, exploring the moments that have taught me valuable lessons about resilience, hope, and the human condition. From the darkness of adversity to the radiance of joy, I share with you the insights that have transformed my perspective and guided me toward a more meaningful life.

These lessons are not universally applicable, nor are they definitive answers. Instead, they are the distilled essence of my imperfect yet genuine experiences. I hope they resonate with you, spark reflection, and inspire your growth journey.

As you read, I encourage you to consider the lessons you've learned. May our shared stories and struggles foster a sense of connection, solidarity, and encouragement.
Join me on this journey, and together, let's explore the wisdom that emerges from life's twists and turns.

TABLE

Dream Big 8
Win Wounded 12
The Power of Being Underestimated 18
Actions Can Speak Louder 20
Faith – The Currency Of Heaven 22
Rise and Shine 25
Tomorrow Is Always A Day Away 27
You Can Have It All, But You Can Not Have It All At Once ... 29
The Anointing Attracts Trouble 31
Wait On Your Promise 33
God Is Revelatory 35
Manage Your Career 37
Compatibility 39
Your Season Of Rejection Is Over 42
Dressing For The Life You Deserve 45
Embracing The Truth 47
An Idea Can Change Your Life 51
Protect Your Gift 54
Let Your Faith Respond 56
God Will Use The Least Likely 60
Seeing Beyond Sight 62
Qualify Yourself Where Favor Places You 64
I Need Wisdom 66
Circles Vs Cycles 68
Decisions 70
Paralyze By Fear 72

Keep It Moving 77
Get Unstuck 80
Not Everyone You Count; 82
You Can Count On.. 82
The Legacy Within: What You Leave In Your Children Matters More Than What You Leave For Them.................................. 86
Unleash Your Voice: The World Is Waiting 93
Planting The Seeds of Your Future... 95
The Power of Your Response 97
Free Yourself And Move On 99
Forgive Yourself First... 101
The Power of Divine Timing 103
Beyond Lack: Living In Divine Provision............................ 105
The Pitfalls of Small Minds In Big Positions 107
Feel. Deal. Heal.. 111
Embracing The Freedom To Change 114
The Process Of Transformation: Embracing Pain, Purpose, and Progress... 119
Embracing Your Authentic Journey 122
The Work In The Shadows 128
The Power of Purpose Over Popularity 131
The Healing Before The Message... 133
The Power of Letting Go 137
Beyond Your Circumstances 140
The Power of Self-Respect 142
The Cost of Compromise 144
Build Your Own World 146
Talent Opens Doors, and Discipline Keeps Them Open 148
Embracing The Limitless Nature of God.............................. 150

Strength Beyond The Breaking Point 153
Cultivating A Habit of Excellence 155
When Work Becomes Purpose 159
Rise Again: The Power of Perseverance 161
The Power Of Thought: Shaping Your Reality 164
When Growth Isn't A Shared Journey 168
The Purpose In The Pit 171
The Condition of Your Heart: The Key To Your Outcome 175
The Miracle In The Breaking Point 178
God Has Your Résumé 182
The Power of Versatility 185
The Weight of Leadership 188
Failure Begins In The Mind 191
The Priceless Rewards of 194
Integrity and Authenticity 194
The Art of Listening — The Secret To Great Speaking 197
The Eternal Student — Staying Relevant As A Teacher 201

DREAM BIG

You possess the inherent right to dream ambitiously and anticipate realizing those dreams.

It is essential not to allow others to undermine your aspirations by suggesting they are overly grand. God often does not bestow a vision that aligns with our current capabilities or is easily attainable. The rationale is that we must cultivate faith to manifest our aspirations. If one's dreams or life vision do not evoke a sense of fear or induce sleeplessness from contemplation of their execution, then you may not be dreaming sufficiently ambitiously.

During my upbringing, my family often reacted with amusement when I articulated my lofty ambitions. They perceived my goals as excessively high and unrealistic. Nonetheless, I received encouragement to persist in my aspirations, mainly from my aunts, who would proudly declare, "That is my nephew who consistently sets his sights high." Despite the discrepancy between my aspirations and the environment in which I was raised, I remained resolute in pursuing grand dreams.

Growing up in our modest two-bedroom wooden home, I expressed to my mother my aspirations to own a spacious house with an attractive lawn and a beautiful backyard. I envisioned marrying at a young age and establishing a family, as I could not imagine raising children outside the bounds of marriage. Despite not having direct examples to guide me, my circumstances did not restrict my aspirations. I actively transformed the negative aspects of my environment into motivation for positive change.

I was profoundly influenced by my grandfather, the late Hubert Hemmings, who successfully founded and managed a business without formal education. His exceptional capacity to dream beyond conventional limits inspired me. As I listened to his narratives of life experiences, struggles, and achievements, I admired his wisdom, which echoed that of King Solomon.

He imparted crucial lessons regarding familial responsibility and the importance of one's presentation in society. He emphasized my duties within the household, reinforcing the notion that I am present to serve, protect, and provide. His counsel included maintaining a polished appearance to ensure I would be treated with respect. He firmly asserted that keeping my word is paramount and that I should never go back on my promises.

My grandfather instilled in me the values of diligence and perseverance as foundational elements for success. He asserted that success becomes attainable when opportunity aligns with ambition. I took his lessons to heart as I embarked on my journey. In 2006, I felt divinely compelled to migrate from Jamaica to Antigua. As a young man moving to a country devoid of immediate family, I was driven by significant dreams and aspirations. However, I remained unaware of the substantial challenges ahead, as my desire to aid my family clouded my awareness of impending obstacles.

Often, success is not immediately observable; trials, setbacks, and challenges frequently obscure it. I have confronted numerous hardships, including exploitation, homelessness, experiences of spiritual disillusionment, and unemployment. Nevertheless, these adversities deepened my relationship with the Lord Jesus Christ and allowed me to understand the essence of faith genuinely. Throughout this journey, I continued to dream ambitiously and ultimately secured a position in the hospitality industry. While the role specifics were initially unclear, I felt immense excitement. This opportunity enabled me to engage with individuals I had never imagined, including prime ministers, royal families, presidents, billionaire entrepreneurs, and various entertainment industry figures. My work led to appearances in television commercials and magazines for the resort where I was employed.

However, my aspirations and visions eventually exceeded the boundaries of my current role and location, prompting me to seek further advancement. I anticipated that my experience and qualifications in the tourism industry would facilitate my employment after working at a prestigious five-star resort; however, I encountered numerous rejections and experienced discrimination based on my skin color. This adversity only intensified my determination to demonstrate my abilities and worth. Ultimately, a professional connection introduced me to the banking sector, prompting me to pursue education in business, culminating in both a bachelor's and master's degree.

Life has afforded me the family, the home, and the children I dreamed about as a young man living in Jamaica because I was relentless in my pursuit of dreaming big and achieving. Dreaming ambitiously about the life you envision and the impact you seek to make on the world is pivotal. Consider who you intend to become. Pursue grand aspirations, for one cannot comprehend their full potential without embracing the challenge of dreaming big.

WIN WOUNDED

*Even though you are wounded,
you're still expected to win.*

You cannot adequately understand Mephibosheth until you have been dropped by someone you've trusted. I don't think you can talk about him adequately until your cripple has a cause that was out of your control. I don't think studying Greek or Hebrew commentaries can enunciate what drives a prince to Lodebar - forced to lie flat on the floor, and for a prince, the grandchild of a King, to say, "I am a dead dog." That kind of depletion and loss of pedigree can only come within the gaze of someone who can relate to that kind of experience of a basement in your life.

That is a part of teaching or preaching that cannot be taught; it must be caught, and it must be personal to you that you are talking about him, but you are drawing from you until you have both become so fused that getting him up off the floor is getting you up off the floor.

Each time I talk about Mephibosheth, the truth is that I am talking about me.

You see, a potency that penetrates the human soul is connectivity, and as you extravagate from the text, the facts are nice to know that you must be willing to talk about your pain, tears, struggle, and re-examine who dropped you and what you would have been if they didn't drop you. The question is, how did you end up in Lodebar when you should be in line for the succession of the next leader? Nevertheless, even though your situation is unimaginable, the only way out is to start crawling.

Having been dropped by my father and then my two trusted pastors has plunged me into a place where ministry no longer resembles the teachings of Jesus. The pain that was inflicted on me left me feeling like the colors of the world had faded away, and I was trapped in a bubble of sorrow and despair. It was like walking in the rain, but the water no longer made me wet.

The feeling of rejection that had always been buried deep in the core of my being and suppressed by my minimal successes was now resurrected and standing before me. I was judged by the reality of my insecurity and inability and the fact that I was a fatherless son. The core of my existence questioned my purpose and lied to me that my gift and calling were outdated and superficial, mere theatrical charisma that grabbed the attention of an audience that had nothing better to do and was acting out of tradition.

Then, I questioned myself; What is in all of this for me? I kept showing up daily with a smile on the outside, but the interior was deteriorating like rust against metal.

The wall I had erected around my heart to guard against being broken tumbled down as the reality set in that I had been hurt by another man I had trusted another leader.

I have been in ministry for many years, and I know that I must keep moving and not sit in my sorrow. However, I also realize that I am human and must allow myself to feel exactly what I was going through.

The way out was crawling until I could walk, but the strength in my limbs and hands failed me. The navigator of my life and ministry broke, and I could no longer see a light at the end of the tunnel.

Despite having traveled extensively throughout the Caribbean, the United States, Canada, and Europe to preach the gospel, pray for the sick, prophesy, and baptize individuals, I have found myself in a metaphorical cave akin to the prophet Elijah. This withdrawal occurred due to an awareness of the unspoken truths within the ministry, which often remain obscured beneath a facade of professionalism. The complexities and challenges of ministry are seldom discussed, as doing so can jeopardize future engagements or opportunities.

Thus, I must summon the resolve, strength, and determination required to continue my journey. I endeavor to move beyond the false narratives that convey insufficiency. I strive to liberate myself from the pain that has confined me and the mental constraints that label me as a reject. Through this process, I have gradually come to believe that the potential within me is far greater than the challenges presented by external circumstances. I remained committed to this journey until my strength was restored, allowing me to reclaim my capacity to walk and run again.

I must admit that moving forward presents its challenges, particularly when one is burdened by the emotional pain stemming from experiences with trusted leaders, friends, and church members. The capacity to rebuild trust often evokes a sense of apprehension, mainly when an individual exhibits excessive kindness or niceness. This reaction prompts a critical evaluation of their intentions, leading to a defensive posture that resists further emotional vulnerability. The internal dialogue often revolves around a desire to avoid repeating past disappointments.

I may not know the specifics of your pain, betrayal, or loss of trust and confidence, but it is essential to recognize that you are destined to win despite these wounds. You must endeavor to win, even if you win wounded.

Triumph Over Trauma

The truth is that our wounds do not define us; our response to them does. We can choose to let our scars strengthen us or suffocate us. You've been hurt, betrayed, or broken. The wounds run deep, and the pain lingers. But what if I told you that your trauma is not a barrier to success? What if I reminded you that you are expected to triumph, not despite your wounds, but because of them?

Resilience is not the absence of scars; it's the courage to wear them with pride. Every wound tells a story of survival, endurance, and strength. Your scars are a testament to your capacity to overcome. Reframe your wounds as lessons learned, opportunities for growth, and self-improvement. View them as strength builders, catalysts for resilience and perseverance, and testimonies to your ability to overcome adversity.

To succeed despite being wounded, acknowledge your pain and recognize the hurt, but don't let it define you. Seek support from people who uplift and encourage. Focus on strengths to rebuild confidence. Celebrate small wins, acknowledging progress no matter how incremental. Prioritize physical, emotional, and mental well-being through self-care.

You are expected to triumph because your story is unique, born from experiences that are yours alone. Your voice matters: share your story to inspire and empower others.

- Your resilience inspires, igniting hope in those around you.
- You are not a victim of your circumstances but a victor over them.
- Your wounds do not disqualify you; they empower you. You are stronger, wiser, and more resilient because of them.

In reflection, consider your wounds and how you can reframe them as strengths. Who supports you on your journey to triumph? What small wins can you celebrate today? Take action by journaling your story, highlighting lessons learned and strengths gained. Seek mentorship from someone who has overcome similar challenges and share your story with someone who needs inspiration.

THE POWER OF BEING UNDERESTIMATED

There's a unique power that comes from being underestimated. It allows you to fly under the radar, observe and listen without being noticed, and plan and strategize without being anticipated.

When others underestimate you, they often let their guard down around you. They may share information, reveal their plans, or show their weaknesses because they don't see you as a threat. This can give you a unique advantage, allowing you to gather intelligence, build alliances, and make moves that others don't see coming.

Moreover, being underestimated can be a powerful motivator. When others doubt your abilities or dismiss your potential, it can fuel your determination to prove them wrong. It can drive you to work harder, to innovate, and to push beyond your limits. You begin to see that the doubts and criticisms of others are not a reflection of your worth or abilities but rather a reflection of their limitations and biases. And with this realization, you can tap into a deep well of inner strength and resilience.

Moreover, being underestimated can be a blessing in disguise. It allows you to operate outside the spotlight without the pressure of expectation or the weight of responsibility. You're free to experiment, take risks, and explore new possibilities without being held back by the doubts and fears of others. And when you finally emerge from the shadows, you can surprise and delight others with your talents, abilities, and achievements.

But the power of being underestimated goes beyond just motivation or strategic advantage. It also speaks to the nature of true strength and resilience. When underestimated, you must rely on your inner resources, trust yourself, and believe in your abilities. This can be a profoundly empowering experience, allowing you to tap into your deepest strengths and discover new capacities within yourself.

So, don't be afraid to be underestimated. Instead, see it as an opportunity to fly under the radar, to gather your strength, and to plan your next move. Remember that true power often lies in being underestimated and that the most significant victories often come from being overlooked.

ACTIONS CAN SPEAK LOUDER

Your behavior can diminish your message. Sometimes, we are saying the correct things, but if your behavior doesn't align with what you are saying, it makes it difficult to hear.

Our actions have a profound ability to either amplify or undermine our words. When our behavior aligns with our message, it resonates deeply with others, inspiring trust and credibility. Conversely, when our actions contradict our words, they can dilute, even nullify, the impact of our message. This disparity between words and actions can lead to skepticism, eroding the confidence others have in us. Consistency between words and actions is crucial.

Our hypocrisy undermines our message if we preach empathy but disregard others' feelings. If we advocate for integrity but compromise our values, our actions speak louder than words. Our behavior becomes the true testament to our character, overshadowing our verbal declarations. Moreover, our actions can convey volumes without uttering a word. Body language, tone, and facial expressions convey subtle yet powerful messages. A warm smile can communicate welcome and inclusivity, while a dismissive glance can convey disdain. Our daily choices and habits also broadcast our priorities and values.

To ensure our actions reinforce our message, we must cultivate self-awareness, recognizing the power of our behavior to either validate or invalidate our words. By aligning our actions with our values and principles, we demonstrate authenticity, building trust and credibility with others.

Ultimately, it's not what we say that defines us but what we do. Our actions are the true messengers of our character, broadcasting our values and intentions to the world.

FAITH – THE CURRENCY OF HEAVEN

Faith – Sees the Invisible, Believes the Unbelievable, Receives the Impossible

Just as currency functions in the physical world to facilitate the purchase of goods and services, faith serves as a form of "currency" that enables individuals to access and engage with the spiritual realm. It is the mechanism through which one can connect with God, receive His blessings, and approach life's challenges with assurance and hope.

This metaphor implies that faith possesses intrinsic value and can be "spent" or invested in several significant ways, including trusting God's promises and provision, adhering to His commands and guidance, pursuing His presence and wisdom, and sharing His love and message with others.

As we "spend" our faith, we can anticipate a corresponding return on investment, manifesting as spiritual growth, peace, joy, and the promise of eternal life.

In other words, faith is the foundation of everything you believe and trust in God for. Your current faith is based on your past experiences. When you have faith, you are entitled to what God promised you. It is not about being arrogant but confident that what God promised will come to pass.

Your faith should be a growing commodity. You must have more faith this year than you had last year and desire what's next.

Faith is illogical because it defies logic. It is hoping for something you cannot see, yet you believe it will happen. Faith sometimes seems senseless because humans tend to align things logically. However, faith is about acting like it's already done because your thoughts, behavior, and posture will activate your faith in action.

Activating your faith is a powerful way to tap into the divine guidance and support always available. It's about more than just believing in the Lord Jesus Christ; it's about putting that belief into action and trusting that God will respond. When you activate your faith, you open yourself to a flow of hope and inspiration to help you navigate even the most challenging situations. You begin to see that everything is working in your favour and that every experience is an opportunity for growth and learning.

So, how do you activate your faith? It starts with a willingness to let go of doubt and fear and to trust in the unknown. It involves cultivating inner peace and calm and being open to guidance and inspiration from within.

You can activate your faith through prayer, meditation, or simply taking a few deep breaths and focusing on the present moment. Remember, faith is not something you must work hard to achieve - it's already within you, waiting to be tapped into and activated. By trusting in yourself and the Lord, you can unlock the power of your faith and experience a more profound sense of purpose, meaning, and fulfillment in your life.

RISE AND SHINE

Rise and Shine is more than just a cheerful greeting - it's a call to action.

As I sip my morning coffee, I'm reminded that every new day is a chance to start fresh, dream big, and make today better than yesterday.

Just like a good cup of coffee can awaken our senses and energize our bodies, a positive mindset can awaken our spirits and lives. So, let's raise our cups (of coffee, tea, or whatever fuels your morning) and toast to a brand-new day full of possibilities, promise, and joy!

Rise and Shine are three simple words with powerful inspiration to transform our lives. When we wake up each morning, we're given a new day full of fresh possibilities and opportunities. The phrase "Rise and Shine" is more than just a cheerful greeting; it's a call to action and a reminder to shake off the slumber of mediocrity and rise to our full potential.

When we choose to Rise and Shine, we consciously start our day with purpose and intention. We commit to tackling challenges head-on, enthusiastically pursuing our passions, and living each moment with gratitude and joy. We rise above the negativity, doubts, and fears that may have held us back in the past. We shine our light, share our gifts with the world, and positively impact those around us.

The powerful inspiration of Rise and Shine is not just limited to our personal lives. It can also be a catalyst for positive change in our communities and the world at large. When we rise and shine our light, we become beacons of hope and inspiration for others. We demonstrate that living a life of purpose, passion, and joy is possible, and we encourage others to do the same. So, let's rise, shine our light, and watch how it can transform our lives and the world around us.

TOMORROW IS ALWAYS A DAY AWAY

The future remains elusive, continually hovering beyond our reach. Depending on your perspective, this notion can elicit comforting and discomforting responses.

On one hand, the assertion that tomorrow is always a day away can provide reassurance. It signifies that there exists time to prepare, reflect, and rejuvenate before confronting the challenges and opportunities that await. It reminds us that we need not possess all answers at present, that it is possible to approach matters incrementally, and that there is a degree of trust to be placed in the unfolding of the future.

Conversely, the idea that tomorrow is always a day away can also evoke discomfort. It underscores the reality that the future is never fully attainable; somewhat, it eludes grasp, akin to sand slipping through one's fingers. This serves as a reminder of the limitations of time, the transient nature of opportunities, and the imperative to maximize the present moment to achieve goals and realize aspirations.

Upon reflection, it becomes evident that tomorrow transcends the concept of a mere day; it is a metaphor for the future itself. It encapsulates the unknown, the unseen, and the unpredictable dimensions of life. This realization highlights that our existence is influenced by forces beyond our control, necessitating that we learn to adapt, evolve, and navigate the unpredictability of fate.

Nonetheless, while acknowledging the uncertainty of the future, it is equally important to recognize the significance of the present moment. We should cultivate the ability to dwell in the here and now, appreciating the beauty and wonder of our surroundings and fostering a sense of gratitude for the blessings and opportunities we currently experience.

As the ancient Greek philosopher Heraclitus stated, "No man ever steps in the same river twice, for it is not the same river, and he is not the same man." While tomorrow is a day away, it simultaneously represents an opportunity for renewal, self-discovery, and recommitment to one's values, passions, and purpose.

Therefore, it is crucial to cherish the present moment with hope and anticipation, even as we look toward the future. It is vital to acknowledge that while tomorrow is always a day away, it also presents an opportunity for growth, learning, and evolution. Ultimately, it is essential to

approach whatever the future holds with courage, resilience, and an open heart.

YOU CAN HAVE IT ALL, BUT YOU CAN NOT HAVE IT ALL AT ONCE

Life is a journey rather than a destination.

Embracing this truth can alleviate the pressure to attain perfection, enabling us to concentrate on making incremental progress.

In today's rapid-paced environment, characterized by a culture of instant gratification, it is easy to fall prey to the notion that one must achieve everything simultaneously. Society inundates us with messages suggesting that possessing the ideal physique, the perfect relationship, an exemplary career, and a flawless life is possible. However, such an achievement is unattainable.

Life inherently involves trade-offs and prioritization. When we devote our attention to certain areas, we may inevitably need to make sacrifices for others. For instance, as you climb the career ladder, extended hours may necessitate reducing time spent with family and friends. Yet, as professional demands evolve, opportunities may arise to scale back work commitments and cultivate personal relationships.

It is essential to acknowledge that life is a progression rather than a series of instant achievements. We should foster incremental improvements according to our goals and values while making deliberate decisions about allocating our time and resources.

Adopting this perspective can be profoundly liberating. By releasing the expectation to have it all, we can focus on appreciating the journey and recognizing small accomplishments. It is evident that life consists of distinct seasons, each offering unique challenges and opportunities.

Therefore, let us take a moment to breathe deeply and relinquish the compulsion to attain everything at once. Instead, let us commit to advancing step by step, trusting that the events unfolding will occur as intended. Remember, you can have it all, but you cannot all at once, and that reality is acceptable.

THE ANOINTING ATTRACTS TROUBLE

The anointing does not shield you from trouble.
It acts like a magnet that attracts trouble.

If you want to identify a person called and anointed by God, they will tell you about their many dangers and hardships. Many seek the anointing, believing they will be protected from their enemies. However, the truth is that David, who God anointed, encountered many troubles.

The anointing on David's life was what caused Saul to want to kill him, and many people who feel threatened by the anointing on someone else's life may attempt to harm them. I experienced this firsthand when I was going through a tough time, and leaders who should have supported me seemed to want me to leave town. I prayed about it and asked God because I was struggling.

God asked me about the purpose of the mongoose in Jamaica and other Caribbean Islands. I answered that the mongoose's purpose was to kill snakes. Then God revealed to me that, despite this, seeing a mongoose on the way somewhere in the Caribbean is often considered bad luck. Why? Because the mongoose usually hangs out in quiet places where snakes are most likely to be found.

Additionally, if a young boy sees a mongoose, he might try to kill it with a stone because he does not understand its purpose.

God then explained that people who don't understand the anointing on your life and its rarity might attempt to harm it. Over the years, I have learned that when people do not understand your calling and the value you bring to the body of Christ, they may reject you, criticize you, spread lies about you, ostracize you, and try to separate you from the body of Christ. But I encourage you to walk in the fullness of God's anointing on your life and live purposefully. The anointing signifies weightiness, splendor, and grandeur. The weight of the anointing on your life terrifies hell. Walk in that anointing and bask in the Lord's glory.

WAIT ON YOUR PROMISE

When a promise is fulfilled, it will be so remarkable that one shall not recall the days before its realization.

A promise is a covenant or a declaration that one will do exactly what one says or something will happen just as pledged. God's promises are not as flippant or casual as we often make. These promises of God are rock-solid and unequivocal commitments made by God, and the recipients of divine promises can have full assurance that what God has spoken will come to pass because God is faithful.

The boundless wisdom of God ensures that each promise made is the optimal assurance that can be provided. God does not require adjustments to His promises; He possesses foreknowledge regarding all outcomes. Promises from God often arise in circumstances where His divine intervention is unmistakable. When God makes a promise, He occupies a unique position; no other individual possesses the authority or capability to actualize these commitments.

According to the Amplified Bible, Joseph exhibited unwavering belief in God's promises, steadfastly maintaining his faith even if he died before their realization. In *Genesis 50:24-26*, Joseph told his brothers, "I am about to die, but God will surely take care of you and bring you up out of this land to the land He promised to Abraham, Isaac, and Jacob." Subsequently, he compelled the sons of Israel (Jacob) to swear an oath, stating, "God will surely visit you and take care of you by returning you to Canaan, and when that occurs, you shall carry my bones up from here."

Joseph's remains were preserved in Egypt until the Exodus to the promised land of Canaan, which transpired approximately two hundred years later. His final burial site was in Shechem, near Samaria, within the parcel of land that Jacob acquired from the sons of Hamor, the father of Shechem *(Joshua 24:32)*. All of Joseph's brothers were interred at this location as well *(Acts 7:15-16)*.

GOD IS REVELATORY

Believers of Christ don't go by situation, but believers go by revelation.

As believers in Christ, we are not meant to be driven by our circumstances or situations. Instead, we're called to live by revelation, the unveiling of God's truth, wisdom, and character in our lives. This means that even amid pain, hardship, or uncertainty, we can focus on the positive, look for the silver lining, and trust that God is working everything out for our good *(Romans 8:28)*.

It's easy to get stuck in the "why" question. Why is this happening to me? Why can't I see a way out? Why is God allowing this to happen? But the truth is, God's ways are not ours, and His thoughts are not ours *(Isaiah 55:8-9)*. Human logic and reasoning cannot explain or figure out God. Instead, He can only be revealed through His Word, prayer, worship, and our experiences.

When we look for the positive amid the pain, we open ourselves up to receiving revelation from God. We begin to see that even in the darkest times, there is always hope, a way forward, and a chance for redemption and restoration. We understand that God is not just a distant observer but an active participant in our lives, working everything out for our good.

So, let's consciously shift our focus away from the situation and onto the revelation. Let's choose to trust that God is good, that He is sovereign, and that He is always working everything out for our good. And remember that even amid pain and uncertainty, we can always find hope and joy in the revelation of God's love and presence in our lives.

MANAGE YOUR CAREER

You are the architect of your career trajectory, the steward of your professional development, and the captain of your path.

As you navigate the complexities of your career journey, it is crucial to identify moments that call for reassessing your course. Recognizing the appropriate time to pursue new challenges, opportunities, and avenues for growth is essential.

To determine whether it is advisable to make a career transition, consider the following indicators: a sense of stagnation, indicating a lack of learning or professional growth in your current position, a decline in challenge and engagement, resulting in feelings of boredom or unfulfilled, the achievement of your existing goals, suggesting readiness for a new set of challenges, a realization that you have outgrown your current role or organization, necessitating the exploration of new opportunities.

Upon acknowledging these signs, assuming control of your career and investigating new possibilities is imperative. The following actions may be beneficial: update and enhance your skills and knowledge to remain competitive within your field, cultivate a robust network and establish connections within your industry, investigate job opportunities that resonate with your personal and professional values, consider further education or specialized training to improve your career prospects.

It is essential to remember that a career is a journey rather than a destination. It is a continual process of growth, learning, and exploration. Ultimately, you are responsible for steering your career in the desired direction.

Therefore, consider this an invitation to pause, summon your courage, and take the initial step toward your next career advancement. You are capable of achieving this objective.

COMPATIBILITY

Not everyone that you are attracted to is compatible with you.

This is a crucial distinction to make, especially regarding romantic relationships. Attraction is often driven by surface-level qualities such as physical appearance, charisma, or charm. However, compatibility goes much deeper. It's about sharing values, personality traits, and long-term goals that create a foundation for a healthy, fulfilling, and sustainable relationship.

Attraction can be fleeting, and it's not uncommon for people to be drawn to someone unsuitable in the long run. This is why it's essential to look beyond the initial attraction and get to know someone deeper. Ask yourself: Do we share the same values and morals? Do we have similar interests and hobbies? Do we communicate effectively and healthily to resolve conflicts?

Compatibility is not just about feeling a spark or a strong connection; it's about being able to build a life together. It's about navigating the ups and downs of life as a team, supporting each other's growth and development, and creating a sense of home and belonging together.

Compatibility is not just about finding someone or something that fits with us; it's about creating a synergy that amplifies our strengths, complements our weaknesses, and brings out our best. When we find compatibility, we experience a sense of harmony, of being in sync with the world around us. It's as if the puzzle pieces of our lives finally fit together, and we can see the complete picture of who we are and what we're capable of.

Compatibility is the foundation upon which trust, intimacy, and communication are built-in relationships. It is the glue that holds us together, even in the face of challenges and disagreements. When we're compatible with someone, we feel seen, heard, and understood in a way that's hard to find elsewhere.

But compatibility isn't limited to romantic relationships. It can be found in friendships, business partnerships, and even our relationships with ourselves. When compatible with our values, passions, and goals, we experience a sense of alignment and purpose that gives us direction and motivation.

Ultimately, the power of compatibility lies in its ability to unlock our full potential. When we find compatibility, we can be our authentic selves, grow and learn together, and create something beautiful and meaningful greater than the sum of its parts.

So, the next time you find yourself drawn to someone, remember that attraction is just the beginning. Take the time to get to know them more profoundly, and ask yourself if you're truly compatible. Your future self will thank you.

YOUR SEASON OF REJECTION IS OVER

*Allow these words to be the balm to th1`e soul,
a reminder that the darkness of rejection
is not permanent.*

Your season of rejection is over. This is more than just a declaration of hope; it's a theological truth rooted in God's very nature. In the biblical narrative, rejection is a recurring theme, but it's never the final word. From Adam and Eve's expulsion from the Garden to the death of the Israelites' wilderness wanderings, rejection is often a precursor to redemption.

In Jesus Christ's life, we see the ultimate rejection—a sinless Savior rejected by the very people He came to save. Yet, in that rejection, we find the most extraordinary redemption the world has ever known—the cross, a symbol of rejection and shame, becomes the instrument of our salvation.

In Christ, we find that our season of rejection is indeed over. The opinions of others no longer define us, nor do the chains of rejection bind us. We are accepted, beloved, and chosen by God Himself. As the apostle Paul writes, "I am convinced that neither death nor life, neither angels nor demons, neither the present nor the future, nor any powers, neither height nor depth nor anything else in all creation, will be able to separate us from the love of God that is in Christ Jesus our Lord" (Romans 8:38-39).

This truth has profound implications for our lives. It means we no longer have to fear rejection because God already accepts us. It means we can take risks, pursue our passions, and live boldly and confidently, knowing that external validation does not define our worth and value.

So, let this truth sink deep into your soul: your rejection season is over. You are accepted, loved, and chosen by God. Walk in the freedom and confidence that comes from knowing this truth, and may it transform every area of your life.

Now, personalize this powerful declaration: "My season of rejection is over." Allow these words to be the balm to the soul, a reminder that the darkness of rejection is not permanent. It's a promise that the season of feeling unwanted, unloved, and unaccepted has ended. Whether it's been a season of romantic, professional, or social rejection, know it's time for a new chapter to begin.

As we emerge from this season of rejection, we're invited to leave behind the shame, the self-doubt, and the fear that may have accompanied it. We're encouraged to rediscover our worth, value, and identity, not in the opinions of others, but in the love and acceptance of our true selves. It's a season of renewal, of restoration, and of rebirth. It's a time to remember that we are enough, just as we are, and that external validation does not define our worth.

So, as we step into this new season, let's do so with hope, faith, and expectation. Let's expect good things to come our way; let's expect to be loved, accepted, and valued for who we are. Let's walk in the confidence that we are worthy of love, acceptance, and success. And let's remember that the rejection season is over, and a brighter, more beautiful season is unfolding before us.

DRESSING FOR THE LIFE YOU DESERVE

Our clothing choices can communicate how we value and respect ourselves and influence how others perceive us.

The way you present yourself to the world reflects how you see yourself. Before you speak a word, your appearance makes an impression before anyone learns about your heart, skills, or dreams. And while true confidence and worth come from within, your clothing choices can express your self-respect, ambition, and identity.

Dressing well isn't about vanity it's about value. When you take the time to present yourself with care, you send a message, not just to others, but to yourself. You affirm that you are worthy of attention, worthy of respect, and worthy of the opportunities you seek. It's not about expensive brands or chasing trends—it's about wearing clothes that make you feel empowered, polished, and prepared for the life you envision.

People respond to how you present yourself. Your attire influences how others perceive you, whether in a professional setting, a social gathering, or everyday routine. A well-dressed person commands attention, not because of superficial appeal, but because their presence reflects self-assurance. People assume you have something valuable to contribute when you show up looking put together. They take you seriously because you take yourself seriously.

But beyond perception, dressing well affects how *you* feel. Have you ever noticed how your confidence shifts when you wear something that makes you feel good? The right outfit can elevate your mindset, inspire productivity, and shift your energy. When you put effort into your appearance, you step into a different level of self-empowerment one where you carry yourself with more purpose, move with more certainty, and engage with the world from a place of strength.

This isn't about dressing for others—it's about dressing for the life you want. Your clothing should align with your vision, goals, and how you want to feel. If you desire success, dress like someone who already embodies it. If you want respect, wear clothes that reflect self-respect. If you seek confidence, present yourself as someone who believes in their worth.

So don't wait for the perfect moment to elevate your style – start now. Choose clothes that reflect your best self. Show up every day as the person you are becoming. When you dress with intention, you don't just change how people see you—you change how you see yourself. And that shift can open doors you never even knew existed.

EMBRACING THE TRUTH

The Hurt isn't my fault, but the healing is my responsibility.

Sitting with our hurt and acknowledging its presence is a courageous and often daunting task. It requires us to confront the pain, fear, and vulnerability we may have been trying to avoid. But this act of acknowledgement allows us to begin healing and making peace with our hurt. When we sit with our hurt, we create space for it to surface, to be felt, and to be understood. We allow ourselves to grieve, to mourn, and to process the emotions that have been locked away.

As we sit with our hurt, we begin to see that it's not just a source of pain but also a teacher. Our hurt can reveal to us the areas where we need to grow, the patterns that need to be broken, and the wounds that need to be healed. By acknowledging our hurt, we can begin to extract its lessons. We can start to see that our hurt is not just a random event but a catalyst for growth, transformation, and liberation. And as we learn the lessons of our hurt, we can begin to make peace with it, forgive ourselves and others, and release the emotional burden we've been carrying.

Making peace with our hurt doesn't mean we forget or deny its impact. It means we've integrated the lessons it taught us and used that knowledge to transform our lives. We've taken the shattered pieces of our hearts and reassembled them into a new, more resilient whole. And as we emerge from this process, we're no longer held captive by our hurt. We're free to live, love, and thrive with a deeper understanding of ourselves and our world.

For many of us, the healing journey begins with acknowledging the hurt inflicted upon us. Whether it's the result of childhood trauma, a toxic relationship, or a painful loss, the hurt is real. And it's not our fault.

But as we embark on the path to healing, we must also acknowledge that we are responsible for our recovery. We cannot wait for others to fix us, apologize, or make amends. We cannot rely on external circumstances to change before we begin to heal.

Healing is an inside job. It requires us to take ownership of our emotions, thoughts, and actions. We must confront our deepest fears, darkest memories, and painful wounds. And it invites us to transform our hurt into healing, our pain into purpose, and our scars into strength.

It's a journey that requires us to turn inward, to confront our deepest wounds, and to nurture our growth. We can't rely on others to fix us or make us whole. We can't wait for external circumstances to change before we begin to heal. Instead, we must take ownership of our healing, recognizing that the power to transform our lives lies within us.

This inside job of healing requires courage, self-awareness, and a willingness to confront our pain. It demands that we be gentle with ourselves, practice self-compassion, and prioritize our well-being. As we embark on this journey, we may encounter resistance, fear, and uncertainty. But with each step forward, we'll discover that we're capable of more than we ever thought possible. We'll learn to trust ourselves, listen to our intuition, and honor our unique healing process.

The beauty of healing is that it empowers us to control our lives. We're no longer victims of circumstance but rather the heroes of our stories. We get to choose how we respond to our challenges, nurture our growth, and create a life that reflects our values and desires. As we heal from the inside out, we'll discover that we're stronger, wiser, and more resilient than we ever thought possible. And we'll emerge from our journey with a deeper understanding of ourselves and a profound appreciation for the transformative power of healing

When we experience hurt, our initial instinct may be to retreat, hide, or numb the pain. But what if we could transform that hurt into a catalyst for growth, transformation, and liberation? What if we could take the darkest moments of our lives and use them as fuel for our most profound evolution? This is the alchemy of healing, where we take the lead of our pain and transmute it into gold.

As we embark on this journey, we begin to see that our hurt is not a weakness but a strength. It's a sign that we're still alive, feeling, and capable of growth. We recognize that our wounds are not liabilities but opportunities for transformation. We learn to approach our pain with curiosity rather than fear and listen to its wisdom. And as we do, we uncover the hidden gifts of our hurt, the lessons that will propel us forward and set us free.

Through this process, we're not erasing our past or denying our pain. We're integrating it, acknowledging its impact, and using it as a springboard for growth. We're taking the shattered pieces of our lives and reassembling them into a new, more resilient whole. And as we emerge from this transformative process, we're no longer the same person who was hurt. We're stronger, wiser, and more compassionate. We're free.

So, the lesson I have learned in this process is that my journey to freedom begins with me. I have to begin the process of healing from within.

AN IDEA CAN CHANGE YOUR LIFE

An idea is the currency of the present.

Ideas are the driving force behind progress, innovation, and change in our current world.

In this sense, ideas are the new currency, replacing traditional forms of wealth and power. Just as money can be used to acquire goods and services, ideas can be used to acquire influence, attention, and resources.

The value of an idea lies in its potential to solve problems, improve lives, and create new opportunities. Ideas can disrupt industries, challenge the status quo, and unite people around a shared vision

In today's fast-paced, rapidly changing world, ideas are more valuable than ever. They are the lifeblood of innovation, entrepreneurship, and social progress. As the adage goes, *"Ideas are the seeds that can change the course of history."*

However, like traditional currency, ideas can be devalued or rendered obsolete if not nurtured, developed, or shared. The currency of ideas requires a supportive ecosystem where creativity, experimentation, and collaboration are encouraged and rewarded.

It reminds us that our ideas can shape the world around us. By valuing, sharing, and acting on our ideas, we can create a brighter, more innovative, and more equitable future for all.

An idea is a spark that can ignite a revolution, a flame that can warm the hearts of humanity, and a light that can illuminate the path to a brighter future. It's a promise of possibility, a gentle nudge toward innovation, and a bold declaration of defiance against the status quo.

The power of an idea lies not in its complexity but in its simplicity. A subtle yet profound shift in perspective can change how we see the world, ourselves, and our place on the earth. Quiet confidence comes from knowing that we have the power to shape our destiny, challenge the norms, and create a new reality.

An idea can be fragile, easily lost in the noise of our busy lives. But it can also be a resilient and relentless force, refusing to be silenced or ignored. It can simmer in the depths of our minds, waiting for the right moment to emerge, to take shape, and to take flight.

The power of an idea lies not only in its ability to inspire but also in its ability to provoke. It can challenge our assumptions, disrupt our comfort zones, and push us to think differently, feel deeply, and act boldly.

Ultimately, the power of an idea lies in its ability to transform us, elevate us, and connect us. It reminds us that we are not just passive observers of the world around us but active participants in shaping its future. We are the dreamers, the thinkers, and the doers who can turn ideas into reality and reality into a better world for all.

PROTECT YOUR GIFT

We are the custodians of our gifts and are responsible for protecting and preserving them.

Protecting your gift is recognizing the immense value and importance of our unique talents, abilities, and passions. It serves as a warning that others may seek to exploit or take advantage of these gifts, potentially leaving us drained and depleted.

Sometimes, people are so excited about your gift that they take your gift and leave you behind, which is a reality many can relate to. We often encounter individuals eager to harness our talents, creativity, or expertise without regard for our well-being or boundaries.

It's essential to remember that our gifts are not separate from ourselves but integral to our identities. When we allow others to exploit or take advantage of our gifts, we risk losing a part of ourselves.

Thus, we must prioritize our nurturing and care. We are the custodians of our gifts and are responsible for protecting and preserving them.

It's important to set healthy boundaries, learn to say no, and prioritize our needs and desires. It means taking the time to rest, recharge, and refocus so that we can continue to nurture and develop our gifts.

By safeguarding our gifts, we are not acting selfishly or egotistically; instead, we are being wise and responsible stewards of the talents and abilities that have been entrusted to us.

Let us prioritize the care and nurturing of our gifts. Our talents are a precious aspect of who we are, and it is our responsibility to protect and preserve them for our benefit and the benefit of those around us.

LET YOUR FAITH RESPOND

Letting our faith respond to our challenges is not always easy, but it's always possible.

Losing sight of our faith is easy amid the pain, hurt, and uncertainty. We may feel like God is distant, silent, or even absent. But the truth is, our faith is not just a feeling but a choice. It's a decision to trust in God's goodness, love, and sovereignty, even when we don't understand what's happening.

When faced with challenges, our faith can respond in one of two ways. We can let our circumstances dictate our faith, or we can let our faith dictate our response to our circumstances. The first approach leads to fear, doubt, and uncertainty. The second approach leads to peace, hope, and confidence.

So, how do we let our faith respond to our challenges? Here are a few key principles to keep in mind:

First, we must remember that our faith is not in our circumstances but in God Himself. We must fix our eyes on Him rather than on our problems. As the Psalmist wrote, *"I will lift my eyes to the hills, from whence comes my help. My help comes from the Lord, who made heaven and earth"* (Psalm 121:1-2).

Second, we must trust God, even when we don't understand what's happening. Trust is not the absence of doubt but the presence of faith. As the Bible says, "Trust in the Lord with all your heart and lean not on your understanding; in all your ways submit to him, and he will make your paths straight" *(Proverbs 3:5-6)*.

Third, we must remember that God always works, even when we can't see it. As the Bible says, *"And we know that in all things God works for the good of those who love him, who have been called according to his purpose" (Romans 8:28)*. We must have faith that God is sovereign, that He is in control, and that He is working everything out for our good.

Finally, we must choose to worship God, even during pain and uncertainty. Worship is not just about singing songs or attending church services; it's about living a life that honors God, even when it's hard. As the Bible says, *"Worship the Lord your God, and serve him only" (Luke 4:8)*.

I recall a challenging period when the organization where my wife and I are employed decided to lay off her entire department. This occurred when mortgage rates were exceptionally high, significantly damaging our budget. My wife needed to retain her employment during this challenging phase. In light of this situation, I confided in a friend about our circumstances, and he expressed his concern due to his understanding of our financial difficulties. He asked about our contingency plans. I responded that our faith must guide us through this adversity. I dedicated considerable time to prayer, presenting our situation before the Lord. I believed in the divine promise we had received and was confident that He would not abandon us or allow our adversaries to revel in our misfortune.

My wife's manager learned of an available internal position and proactively contacted the vice president of that division, advocating for my wife and requesting an interview. According to the layoff terms, my wife had sixty days from the date of notification to secure internal employment. As that deadline approached, it became urgent for her to seek alternatives before she was required to accept the layoff package.

She attended the interview with the vice president, who was notably impressed by her professionalism, presentation, and demeanor. The discussion primarily centered around her personality rather than the role specifics, indicating that the light of God within her had captured the interviewer's attention. After several days of anxious waiting and time running short, my wife received communication from human resources, informing her that she would need to sign the layoff package if she did not secure a position.

On the final day of the deadline, my wife requested that I sign the necessary documentation as a witness, a human resources requirement. I complied, emphasizing that my signature was merely a formality, but I firmly believed that her success had already been ordained. While she was scanning the documents to send to HR, the phone rang. The vice president called to congratulate her and confirm that they would be proceeding with her for the new role. Remarkably, this occurred just two hours before the deadline.

The lesson I have learned in this moment is that when your faith responds, your answer will always be delivered on time.

Letting our faith respond to our challenges is not always easy, but it's always possible. When we trust God, worship Him, and remember He is always working, we can experience peace, hope, and confidence, even amid pain and uncertainty. So, let your faith respond to the challenges you're facing today. Choose to trust God and watch Him work everything out for your good.

GOD WILL USE THE LEAST LIKELY

Our human expectations, biases, or limitations do not limit God.

When we think of someone least likely to accomplish something, we often imagine someone who lacks the typical qualifications, skills, or experience. They may be overlooked, underestimated, or even marginalized by others. However, God's ways are not ours, and He often uses those considered least likely to achieve great things.

The Power of God's Sovereignty

God will use the least likely to do the unlikely, which shows His sovereignty and His ability to choose whomever He desires to accomplish His purposes. Our human expectations, biases, or limitations do not limit God. He can use someone who appears weak, unqualified, or insignificant to achieve something extraordinary.

The Bible contains examples of God using the least likely individuals to achieve great things.

- **David and Goliath:** David, a young shepherd boy, was considered the least likely to defeat the giant Goliath. However, with God's help, David emerged victorious.

- **Moses:** Moses, a stuttering former fugitive, was unlikely to lead the Israelites out of slavery.

However, God chose Moses for this task, and he became one of the most outstanding leaders in biblical history.

- **The Disciples:** Jesus chose a group of unlikely individuals, including fishermen, tax collectors, and revolutionaries, to be His disciples. Despite their lack of formal education or training, they changed the world.

The statement "God will use the least likely to do the unlikely" has several implications and applications:

- Don't underestimate others: We should never underestimate someone's potential based on their appearance, background, or abilities. God can use anyone to achieve great things.
- Don't underestimate yourself: We should recognize that God can use us, regardless of our perceived limitations or weaknesses. We should be open to God's call and willing to step out in faith.
- Look for opportunities to serve: We should seek opportunities to serve and support those around us, especially those considered *"least likely"* to achieve great things.

SEEING BEYOND SIGHT

What you see with your eyes doesn't often support what you see with your spirit.

What you see with your eyes will not always align with what you know in your spirit. Life presents challenges that make faith seem irrational, doors that won't open, circumstances that don't change, and prayers that seem unanswered. If we rely only on what is visible, we can become discouraged, believing that what we see is all there is. But faith reminds us that there is more. God is always working behind the scenes, even when we cannot see it with our physical eyes.

There is a reason why God sometimes allows us to experience seasons of uncertainty. When He removes our reliance on what is seen, He invites us to develop a deeper trust in Him. Spiritual vision is not about what is happening *around* us but what God is doing *within* us. It is the ability to see past obstacles and into divine purpose, to believe in breakthroughs before they manifest, and to trust that God's plan is unfolding even when it doesn't look like it.

Consider how often in Scripture God called people to trust Him beyond what their eyes could see. Abraham was promised to be the father of nations while he was still childless. Joseph saw dreams of greatness while sitting in a prison cell. The Israelites were told of a land flowing with milk and honey while they wandered in the wilderness. Every great move of God required someone to trust beyond what their natural sight could comprehend. Their faith was the bridge between what *was* and what *would be*.

This is why spiritual vision is essential. The enemy wants to distract you with what looks like failure, lack, or delay, so you lose faith in what God has already spoken. But just because you don't *see* it yet doesn't mean it's not coming. God is not limited by what is visible—He works in dimensions you cannot yet perceive.

If God has removed your ability to rely on sight, it is because He is strengthening your ability to rely on Him. Trust that He sees what you cannot. Lean into His promises, even when circumstances seem to contradict them. Pray for eyes that see beyond the natural, ears that hear His voice above the noise, and a heart that believes even when nothing makes sense.

Because when you learn to see with your spirit, no setback, delay, or obstacle can shake your faith. You will walk confidently, not because of what is in front of you, but because of Who is leading you. And in time, what you believe in faith will become the reality you see with your eyes.

QUALIFY YOURSELF WHERE FAVOR PLACES YOU

Favour isn't fair.

Several years ago, I experienced a profound moment of inspiration as I began my career in corporate banking. Although I had no previous experience in the banking sector, I consistently prayed for an opportunity in this field, which I perceived as a noble profession in which I wished to participate. A client I had engaged with during my tenure at a resort made a valuable connection for me after I relocated to Canada, where I initially encountered challenges in securing employment, ultimately facilitating my entry into the banking industry.

During one workday, I received an insightful message in my spirit: "Qualify yourself where favor places you."

Our preparation, diligent effort, and commitment can position us for opportunities we may not have previously been adequately equipped to handle.

It encompasses the unforeseen opening of doors, the unsolicited phone calls that can be pivotal, or serendipitous encounters that foster new connections.

However, favor alone is insufficient. We must also take the initiative to qualify ourselves to receive and adequately capitalize on the opportunities to favor presents. This entails developing our skills, enhancing our character, and preparing ourselves for the challenges and responsibilities that accompany new prospects.

By qualifying ourselves, we demonstrate our responsibility, reliability, and commitment to excellence. We convey that we deserve the favor extended to us and are ready to maximize the opportunities that will present themselves.

We must be deliberate about qualifying ourselves and preparing for the forthcoming favor. Let us invest in skill development, character building, and overall positioning for success. When favor affords us the opportunity, let us be poised to seize it with both confidence and excellence.

I NEED WISDOM

Wisdom transcends the mere accumulation of knowledge or understanding.

I sought the Lord for the gift of wisdom akin to Solomon's. In response to my prayers, I experienced a vision in which the Lord conveyed a significant message:

"A man filled with wisdom must wisely behave himself."

Initially, I did not fully grasp the meaning of this message; however, I later understood that God was telling me about the importance of living a life aligned with one's values, principles, and acquired knowledge.

Wisdom transcends the mere accumulation of knowledge or understanding; it encompasses the application of that wisdom in practical and meaningful ways. The essence of this message was to emphasize that I am imbued with wisdom. I must demonstrate this quality through my actions, decisions, and behaviour.

This necessitates mindfulness in our conduct across all facets of life, from personal relationships to professional obligations. It requires intentionality regarding the choices we make, the words we articulate, and the actions we undertake.

Exhibiting wise behaviour demands self-awareness, self-discipline, and self-regulation. It entails managing our emotions, controlling impulses, and making decisions congruent with our values and objectives.

When we behave wisely, we cultivate respect and trust among peers and those around us. We present ourselves as responsible, reliable, and trustworthy, demonstrating a commitment to integrity, honesty, and authenticity.

Ultimately, wise behaviour reflects our character and dedication to living a purposeful and meaningful life. It serves as a poignant reminder that wisdom is not solely a possession but a practice that must be actively demonstrated in our daily actions.

As the ancient Greek philosopher Aristotle aptly stated, "We are what we repeatedly do. Excellence, then, is not an act but a habit." We must strive to cultivate wisdom as a habitual practice and to embody wise conduct in every aspect of our lives.

CIRCLES VS CYCLES

Don't confuse circles with your cycles.

The individuals and circumstances in our lives do not always accurately represent our personal growth or development.

Circles refer to the various relationships and environments encompassing us, including friends, family, colleagues, and social networks. These circles can serve as sources of support and encouragement; however, they can also become draining or toxic.

Conversely, "cycles" pertain to our patterns and habits, encompassing our thought processes, emotional reactions, and behavioral tendencies. Cycles may be constructive and empowering, but they can manifest as unfavorable and limiting.

The challenge arises when there is a misidentification between circles and cycles. You may erroneously attribute your difficulties to the people and situations surrounding you when the root of the issue may reside within your cycles.

For instance, you might attract detrimental relationships due to negative thought patterns or feelings of low self-worth. Additionally, struggles with anxiety or depression may stem from maladaptive emotional responses to stress or trauma.

When you conflate your circles with your cycles, you may find yourself in a pattern of blame and victimhood, feeling powerless to change your circumstances, believing that external factors dictate your life.

However, you can begin to take ownership of your life upon recognizing that cycles are within your control. You can identify and challenge detrimental thought patterns, emotional responses, and behavioral habits. This awareness allows you to break free from cycles that have hindered progress and to establish new, empowering patterns that foster personal growth and well-being.

It is imperative to differentiate between circles and cycles. By owning your life and acknowledging that cycles are manageable, you can liberate yourself from limiting patterns and construct a more promising and empowering future.

DECISIONS

You are reminded of your ability to shape your life through intentional decision-making.

There is an old man or woman in you, depending on the decisions that you make now as a young man or woman. In other words, you are born looking like your parents but die looking like your decisions. Your decisions can undoubtedly alter your future.

When you are born, you inherit various physical characteristics, traits, and tendencies influenced by genetics and upbringing. However, as you mature, you begin to make choices that can significantly alter your life trajectories. Conversely, you can die looking like your decision based on your choices, which can ultimately define your identity. These decisions can influence physical health, mental well-being, relationships, and overall quality of life.

This perspective extends beyond mere physical appearance; it encompasses the individual you become due to your choices. For instance;

- Do you prioritize their health or neglect it?
- Do you cultivate meaningful relationships or allow them to deteriorate?
- Do you pursue your passions, or do you settle into a life of mediocrity?

Significantly, decisions can indeed transform future outcomes. You possess the power to determine the kind of life you wish to lead, the person you aspire to become, and the legacy you intend to leave.

Nevertheless, this power entails a responsibility to acknowledge personal choices. You cannot attribute the outcomes of your life solely to circumstances, upbringing, or genetics. It is essential to accept responsibility for your decisions and recognize their consequences.

Ultimately, this serves as a call for introspection and self-reflection. It encourages critical examination of current choices and their potential impact on the future. You are reminded of your ability to shape your life through intentional decision-making.

Therefore, it is advisable to take a moment to reflect on your current choices. It is crucial to consciously choose wisely, as these decisions will ultimately shape your identity and future.

PARALYZE BY FEAR

The paralysis instigated by fear can adversely affect your faithfulness to God.

Fear is one of the most potent forces that can paralyze a person, preventing them from moving forward. It whispers doubts, magnifies risks, and keeps us in a cycle of hesitation and inaction. But beyond its impact on our ambitions and dreams, fear has a more profound and more dangerous effect—it hinders our faithfulness to God. When fear takes root in our hearts, it can cause us to question God's plans, delay our obedience, and ultimately rob us of the blessings of walking boldly in faith.

Fear: The Silent Faith Killer

Fear and faith cannot coexist. Where fear reigns, faith is diminished. We see this throughout Scripture—when people allow fear to control them, they either disobey God, delay His plans or completely miss out on what He has for them. One of the most well-known examples is the Israelites in the wilderness.

After God delivered them from slavery in Egypt, He promised them a land flowing with milk and honey. But when the spies returned with reports of giants in the land *(Numbers 13:32-33)*, fear overtook faith. Instead of trusting his homeland without knowing his final destination *(Hebrews 11:8)*. He moved, and God directed. The same applies to us.

3. **Pray for Boldness, Not Just Clarity** – We often pray for clear answers when we need courage. God may not always reveal every detail, but He will equip us with the strength to move forward. Ask Him for the boldness to obey, even when the way is uncertain.

4. **Surround Yourself with Faith Builders** – Fear grows in isolation, but faith is strengthened in the community. Surround yourself with people who encourage, uplift, and remind you of God's truth when fear tries to creep in.

5. **Declare God's Word Over Your Fear** – Replace fearful thoughts with faith-filled declarations. When anxiety rises, declare *2 Timothy 1:7: "For God has not given us a spirit of fear but of power and love and a sound mind."* When doubt comes, stand on *Isaiah 41:10*: *"Fear not, for I am with you; be not dismayed, "for I am your God. I will strengthen you, yes, I will help you, I will uphold you with My righteous right hand."*

Faith Over Fear: The Key to Moving Forward

God has called you to more than a life of hesitation and regret. The enemy uses fear to keep you from stepping into your God-given destiny, but you have the power to overcome it. Every great move of God requires faith, and faith requires trust. The question is not whether fear will come it will. The question is: **Will you allow it to stop you?** Don't let fear paralyze your faithfulness. Choose trust. Choose obedience. Choose to move forward, even when you don't have all the answers. Because when you step out in faith, you will see God move in ways you never imagined. Keep walking. Keep trusting. **And no matter what don't let fear hold you back.**

KEEP IT MOVING

Every line, every scar, and every change is a mark of survival, experience, and transformation.

We keep trying to hold on to the last season we were in instead of embracing the one we are in now. But life is not meant to be lived in rewind. Every season serves its purpose some to build us, some to break us, some to teach us, and others to elevate us. The key is embracing each one fully, knowing it shapes us for what's next.

Embrace your season, your stages, and your ages. Too often, we resist change because we mourn what it used to be. But resisting does not stop time, and clinging to the past does not restore it. We are constantly evolving, and we must not despise the transition. If we do, we will miss the beauty in the wrinkles on our skin, the grey hairs that whisper stories of wisdom, and the deeper understanding that only time can provide. Instead, we Botox our way through life, trying to erase the evidence of growth, pretending we can hold on to a version of ourselves that no longer exists. But the truth is, every line, every scar, every change is a mark of survival, experience, and transformation.

Overcoming the Obstacles of Moving Forward

I know that moving forward is easier said than done. It requires breaking free from the chains of comfort, fear, and doubt. But sometimes, we are held back by the pain of the past, the weight of regret, or the fear of what's ahead. But here's the truth: progress is impossible without change, and change is often uncomfortable.

Fear of the Unknown – One of the biggest reasons people stay stuck is the fear of what's next. The "what ifs" creep in—What if I fail? What if it doesn't work out? But what if it does? What if this next step is exactly what you need? The only way to know is to move.

Emotional Baggage – Unhealed wounds, past disappointments, and lingering resentment can weigh you down. Forgiveness, whether for yourself or others, doesn't mean forgetting; it does mean freeing yourself from the chains of bitterness. Release what no longer serves you so you can move forward with a lighter heart.

Comfort in Familiarity – Staying in the same place, even if it's not serving you, can feel safer than stepping into the unknown. But growth doesn't happen in comfort zones. The longer you stay in a place that no longer fits you, the more you shrink yourself to stay there.

Fear of Failure – Understand that failure is not the opposite of success but a stepping stone toward it. Every successful person has failed, but they keep going. Don't let the fear of falling keep you from flying.

Moving on in life doesn't mean you forgot what happened. It doesn't mean the pain, the loss, or the lessons vanish. It means you have accepted what happened and decided not to let it define, drain, or rob you of the life ahead. Acceptance is not a weakness it is a strength. It is choosing to carry the wisdom forward without carrying the weight of the past.

So, keep putting one foot in front of the other. Keep evolving. Keep growing. Push past the obstacles. Keep it moving. Because life is still happening, you owe it to yourself to show up for it.

GET UNSTUCK

*You will never know what's behind the
next door until you move and open it.*

One can easily choose to remain in a space that no longer serves you or accommodates your growth simply because of the fear of the unknown and unfamiliar. It's easy to convince yourself that staying put is the safer option. The mind whispers, what if the next step is worse? What if I fail? What if I lose everything? And so, you remain stuck—not because you cannot move, but because you have conditioned yourself to fear what lies ahead.

You are terrified of disrupting the dysfunction of being comfortable, so you pay the price of waking up each morning feeling unfulfilled and in pain. You keep spending day after day in a space that no longer fits you, like wearing shoes that have grown too tight but refusing to take them off. The discomfort becomes familiar, and familiarity feels safer than change—even when it's suffocating you.

Then, without realizing it, your stagnation begins to affect those around you. The people in your inner circle start to tolerate you instead of truly seeing and supporting you. The energy shifts. The enthusiasm they once had for your dreams, conversations, and presence begins to wane because they can sense what you are too afraid to admit: You are stuck.

This is a clear sign that it is time to move time to explore the unknown, no matter how terrifying it may seem. You will never know what's behind the next door until you move and open it. Staying in a place that no longer serves you is not just a disservice to yourself—it's a slow betrayal of the life you were meant to live.

So today, I permit you to take that first step: start that business, buy that house, find that new job, leave that relationship, enroll in that course, move to that city, and do what is conducive to your growth, fulfillment, and happiness.

You owe it to yourself to move forward. You owe it to yourself to get unstuck.

NOT EVERYONE YOU COUNT; YOU CAN COUNT ON

Not everyone who claps for you wants to see you win.

Life has a way of revealing the truth about the people around us. We often assume that those we hold dear family, friends, colleagues will be the ones to support us when we need them most. We count them in our circles, in our plans, and in our moments of vulnerability. But when the storm hits, when life becomes heavy, we realize a sobering truth: *not everyone you count, you can count on.*

The Illusion of Loyalty

Loyalty is a word we use freely, but its true meaning is often misunderstood. We expect it to be automatic, assuming that proximity equals reliability. Just because someone has been in your life for years does not mean they are equipped or willing to stand with you in the trenches. Some people are present for convenience, personal gain, or simply because they have never had a reason to leave. But when life tests your foundation, when the weight of your struggles presses down on you, you will see who remains standing.

Not everyone you count on will be there when it truly matters. This harsh reality forces us to confront the fragile nature of human relationships. We invest in people, forging bonds and building trust, only to discover that some connections are built on shifting sands. The ones we thought would stand by us through life's storms may vanish when the winds howl loudest.

Jesus Himself experienced this. He handpicked twelve disciples, walked with them, taught them, and shared His intimate moments. Yet when the pressure mounted, when the cross loomed near, betrayal and abandonment were close behind. Judas, whom He had counted as one of His own, sold Him for thirty pieces of silver. Peter, who swore loyalty, denied Him three times. The remaining disciples scattered in fear. If even Jesus, who chose with divine wisdom, had those in His circle who failed Him, why do we think we are exempt?

Who's Really in Your Corner?

Not everyone who claps for you wants to see you win. Some are only with you because of what they receive from the connection. Others stay because it's easy until sacrifice is required. Here's how to recognize who you can truly count on:

- **Watch Who Stays in the Storm** – Fair-weather friends will disappear when life gets rough. The ones who remain, who stand beside you without expecting anything in return, are the ones you can count on.
- **Observe Who Celebrates Your Success** – Some people are comfortable with you if you remain on their level. But when you grow, achieve, or change, their energy shifts. Faithful supporters celebrate with you, not resent you.
- **Pay Attention to Actions, Not Just Words** – Promises mean nothing without follow-through. People will tell you they are there for you, but their consistent actions reveal their true loyalty over time.
- **Accept That Some People Are Seasonal** – Some connections are meant for a chapter, not the whole *"story. Letting go of relationships that no longer serve your growth is not bitterness it's wisdom"*

Finding Strength in Disappointment

Yet, in these moments of betrayal and disappointment, we discover our spirits' resilience. We learn to discern the genuine from the superficial, to cherish the few who prove steadfast, and to find strength in our unshakable core. Pain has a way of clarifying what truly matters and who truly belongs.

Ultimately, it's not the number of people we count on that matters but the quality of those relationships and the depth of our character. The people who remain the ones who show up in your darkest moments, cheer for you in your brightest, and stand firm through all the in-between are the ones worth holding onto.

So, count wisely. And when people show you who they are, believe them.

THE LEGACY WITHIN: WHAT YOU LEAVE IN YOUR CHILDREN MATTERS MORE THAN WHAT YOU LEAVE FOR THEM

When you die, as a parent, it is not the inheritance you leave for your children that will make them excel, but what you leave in them that will make them great. What is in them is greater than what they possess.

As parents, we often feel the weight of responsibility to provide for our children. We work tirelessly to give them a good life, ensuring they have opportunities, financial security, and perhaps even an inheritance to fall back on. However, the greatest gift we can give our children is not measured in dollars or possessions.

When you die, it is not the inheritance you leave for your children that will make them excel, but what you leave in them will make them great.

Material wealth can be spent, lost, or mismanaged. Houses, cars, and bank accounts can fade away. But the values, wisdom, and strength you plant within your children will carry them further than any material asset ever could.

The Power of What's Within

The world often teaches that success is about what you accumulate, but true greatness is about what's inside you. **What is in them is more significant than what they possess.** This means that resilience, integrity, faith, and wisdom are far more valuable than any financial inheritance. These tools will shape their decisions, guide them through life's challenges, and sustain them even when all else is lost. Think of history's most significant figures—leaders, inventors, and visionaries. Most were not born into riches, yet they changed the world. Why? Because what was *in* them—determination, creativity, character—was greater than what they *had* at any given moment.

The Difference Between Legacy and Wealth

Wealth can create comfort, but legacy creates character. A financial inheritance can set your children up for temporary stability, but the values you instill in them will determine how they use them. Money without discipline leads to recklessness, and opportunity without wisdom leads to failure. However, a child who has been taught resilience, hard work, and integrity will not only build upon what they receive but will create something more extraordinary.

Consider two families:
- One leaves millions in inheritance, but the children lack discipline and wisdom. Within a few years, the money is gone, and they are left with nothing.
- The other family leaves little wealth, but their children were raised with strong values, faith, and perseverance. Over time, they build their success, overcoming obstacles because they are equipped with the right mindset.

Which legacy is greater?

What Will Your Children Carry from You?

What would your children say you left in them if today were your last day? Would they tell you left them with faith, courage, wisdom, and a strong work ethic? Or would they remember only the material things you provided?

Your legacy is built in the everyday moments—how you teach them to handle adversity, model kindness and humility, and show them the importance of faith. It's in the lessons you teach when no one is watching, the principles you stand by, and the love you pour into them.

Building a Lasting Legacy
- **Instill Values, Not Just Comfort** – Teach them the importance of honesty, hard work, and integrity. These qualities will open doors that money never could.
- **Show Them Resilience** – Life will bring challenges. Show them how to rise after a fall and keep going when things get complicated.
- **Give Them Faith** – Money may run out, but faith sustains. Instil in them a deep trust in God and a purpose greater than themselves.
- **Teach Them Financial Wisdom** – If you leave them wealth, ensure they have the discipline to manage it wisely. Money without wisdom is a burden, not a blessing.
- **Be Present**—Time is the most significant inheritance. The lessons learned in simple, everyday moments will be their foundation.

As parents, our goal should not be to leave our children something to live *on* but something to live *by*. What we leave in them will shape their destiny, outlast our years, and create a ripple effect for future generations.

Lessons Learned

True Wealth is Internal, Not External – Material inheritance can be lost, but values, wisdom, and character will guide a person for a lifetime. What's in a child is more valuable than what they possess. Parents must prioritize shaping their children's mindset and character over merely providing financial security.

Legacy is Greater Than Wealth – Leaving a financial inheritance is helpful but insufficient. Instilling faith, resilience, integrity, and wisdom ensures that children can navigate life successfully, regardless of their financial status. True success comes from creating opportunities, making wise decisions, and persevering through challenges.

Character Determines Success – Hard work, perseverance, and discipline are the keys to a meaningful and successful life. Without these qualities, even a large inheritance can be squandered. Teaching children responsibility and accountability prepares them to manage whatever resources they acquire, whether wealth or opportunities.

Resilience is the Greatest Gift - Teaching children how to rise after failure, handle adversity, and move forward equips them for any challenge. Money can provide temporary relief, but resilience ensures long-term stability. Parents should model perseverance and instill in their children the mindset that setbacks are growth opportunities.

Faith Provides Stability – Money may come and go, but faith in God and a strong moral foundation will sustain children through life's ups and downs. Teaching children to trust in something greater than themselves helps them develop inner peace, wisdom, and a sense of purpose that transcends financial or material success.

Parental Influence Shapes Generations – Parents' lessons, habits, and values impact their children and future generations. A strong foundation today leads to a better tomorrow. Parents' principles will echo through time, shaping families, communities, and society.

Time and Presence Matter More Than Possessions – The most lasting lessons come from shared moments, conversations, and experiences. Being present in a child's life is the most significant investment. Children may forget gifts and material things, but they will always remember the wisdom, love, and guidance their parents provided.

Leaving a financial inheritance is helpful, but it is not enough. Instilling faith, resilience, integrity, and wisdom ensures that children can navigate life successfully, regardless of their financial status. True success comes from creating opportunities, making wise decisions, and persevering through challenges.

So, ask yourself: **What am I depositing into my children that will last beyond my lifetime?** Because, in the end, their true greatness won't come from what they possess but from what they carry within them.

UNLEASH YOUR VOICE: THE WORLD IS WAITING

It's easy to believe that our contributions don't matter, that our voices will be lost in the noise.

We all have a responsibility to leverage our voices, and we can't stop until our voices are heard. The power of expression is not a privilege; it's a responsibility. Too often, we silence ourselves out of fear; fear of rejection, fear of judgment, or fear of stepping outside of what is comfortable. But greatness is never born in comfort. It thrives in the spaces where we dare to be seen, heard, and felt.

Think about it: what if the greatest singers had never sung? What if the most influential speakers had remained silent? What if the most brilliant artists had never dared to pick up a brush? The world would be robbed of their genius. And the same is true for you.

You have something inside you that the world needs: a message, a story, a talent, and a perspective that no one else can offer in quite the same way. But if you keep it locked up inside the convenience of a small group of people, only sharing your light in safe spaces, you will never know how bright you can truly shine.

So, **keep talking until somebody listens.** Speak up in meetings, share your thoughts, and tell your story even when you think no one is paying attention. The right ears will hear you when the time is right.

Keep singing until somebody claps. Whether your song is a melody, movement, poetry, or a purpose-driven mission, keep going. Your voice matters. Someone, somewhere, is waiting for exactly what you have to offer.

Keep painting until somebody stares. Whatever your gift is writing, designing, building, or innovating, put it out there. Don't hide your talents in the shadows of self-doubt. The world is waiting to see you and *needs* to see you.

It's easy to believe that our contributions don't matter, that our voices will be lost in the noise.

But history tells us otherwise. Every revolution, movement, and masterpiece started with someone refusing to stay silent or hide their gift.

Choose to step outside of what you know. Embrace the discomfort of being seen. Speak, create, and inspire. The world is waiting to hear what you have to say.

PLANTING THE SEEDS OF YOUR FUTURE

Your thoughts are seeds, and your actions are seeds. The words you speak, the habits you build, and the choices you make plant something in your life.

Every seed is a potential fruit. Your life, your success, your habits, and your future they all begin with the seeds you plant today. If you are not pleased with the fruit you are harvesting, it's time to look at the seeds you've sown. People often wonder where certain behaviors, lifestyles, and attitudes come from. They look at their struggles, setbacks, and disappointments and ask, *"Why is my life this way?"* But the truth is simple: It all starts with a seed.

Your thoughts are seeds. Your actions are seeds. The words you speak, the habits you build, and the choices you make plant something in your life. And just like a farmer cannot expect apples from an orange tree, you cannot expect success if you have planted seeds of procrastination, doubt, and negativity.

So, if you want to change your life situation, start planting new seeds. Choose your seeds with intention if you want a future filled with abundance; plant seeds of discipline, hard work, and perseverance. Plant seeds of kindness, honesty, and patience if you want more substantial relationships. Plant seeds of self-care, good nutrition, and exercise to be healthier.

Remember, **you will harvest what you plant** not immediately but inevitably. Growth takes time, and patience is key. No farmer plants a seed today and expects a tree tomorrow. But they trust the process. They water the soil, remove the weeds, and wait for the harvest.

The same applies to your life. If you stay consistent in planting good habits, values, work, and decisions, you will eventually see the results. The harvest will come.

Also, remember that **whatever you plant, you shall reap.** If you sow bitterness, you will reap resentment. If you plant excuses, you will harvest regret. But if you plant faith, effort, and a positive mindset, you will reap a full, meaningful, and prosperous life with possibilities.

THE POWER OF YOUR RESPONSE

Your response has power. It can either start a conflict or start a conversation.

Life will test you. People will push your buttons, misunderstand you, and sometimes even disrespect you. And in those moments, when you want to go low, when you feel the urge to lash out, curse someone out, or strike back, it's all about your ego. It's about seeking revenge for the things that have happened to you.

But here's the truth: **What happens to you doesn't define who you are.** Life's challenges, betrayals, and disappointments may shape you, but they don't have the final say in your character. What truly defines you is how you *respond*.

Your response has power. It can either start a conflict or start a conversation, feed negativity or bring about change. The choice is always yours.

Now, this doesn't mean you have to be passive. Being the bigger person doesn't mean letting people walk all over you, ignoring injustice, or pretending that wrongs don't exist. Being the bigger person means keeping your equilibrium. It means standing firm in your values, addressing the situation with wisdom, and choosing words that uplift rather than tear down.

I get it; it's not always the easiest thing to do. When emotions run high, it's tempting to react rather than respond. But remember: **Character matters.**

Somebody is watching you. Someone looks up to you. Maybe it's a younger sibling, a child, a friend, or a stranger who admires how you carry yourself. And in the heat of the moment, when you decide how to react, you're not just shaping your reputation; you're influencing the people you inspire.

So, pause and reflect. What light are you trying to shine? What words are you choosing to say? Because every moment of frustration is an opportunity to either add to the noise or to lead by example.

Think about these things. Then, choose wisely.

FREE YOURSELF AND MOVE ON

You deserve a love that doesn't require you to question your place in someone's life.

Relationships are built on trust, commitment, and mutual respect. When two people agree to be together in a monogamous relationship, they are making a promise not just to love each other but to honour the bond they share. So, if someone cheats, it has nothing to do with you. It does not reflect your worth, beauty, or ability to love. It is a reflection of their choices, integrity, and inability to honour the commitment they made.

When someone violates a relationship's trust, they reveal something about themselves, not you. It tells you that they lack the integrity to stand by their word. And integrity is everything. If people cannot be truthful in their closest relationships, how can they be trusted in anything else?

You should never blame yourself for someone else's betrayal. You should never question your value because another person failed to be faithful. Instead, you should recognize the truth: that person has an issue with integrity and honesty that has *nothing* to do with you.

And once you see it for what it is, the choice becomes clear—you should choose against a relationship with someone who surrenders their integrity so quickly. Cheating does not just break promises; it shows you who you are. Believe them.

The best thing you can do for yourself? Free yourself and move on. Please do not waste your energy trying to understand or change their reasons. That's not your burden to carry. Your responsibility is to yourself—to heal, grow, and step forward into a future where honesty, loyalty, and genuine love exist.

You are worthy of a love that doesn't require you to question your place in someone's life. Let go of what no longer serves you and make room for something better.

FORGIVE YOURSELF FIRST

Healing starts with you. So let go of the guilt and shame and step into the future with a renewed sense of self-love.

Forgiveness is one of the hardest things to give—especially when the wound runs deep. When someone hurts you, demeans you, or continuously takes advantage of your kindness, it's natural to hold on to anger and resentment. But what happens when you *can't* seem to forgive?

Forgive yourself first

Before forgiving the person who hurt you, you must understand your role. That doesn't mean blaming yourself for someone else's actions—it means recognizing that, in every relationship you've ever had, whether romantic or platonic, you *chose* to participate.

That choice may have been made out of love, hope, loneliness, or even the belief that things would get better. But regardless of the reason, the first step to healing is acknowledging that you played a part—not in their behavior, but in staying, excusing, and believing when all signs pointed otherwise.

And that's okay. **You're human.**

Everyone comes into your life for a reason, a season, or a lifetime. Some people teach you lessons; some help you grow, and some remind you of what you should never settle for again. If you only focus on *what they did*—on the external factors—you miss the opportunity to look inward, reflect, and truly understand what's happening inside *you*.

So, before anything else, go back. Look at the moments where you ignored your gut, silenced your needs, and stayed in something unhealthy because it was familiar. And then, **forgive yourself.**

Forgive yourself for believing in someone who couldn't give you what you deserved. Forgive yourself for staying when you knew you should have left. Forgive yourself for giving chance after chance to someone unwilling to change.

Forgive yourself for *not knowing then what you know now*.

Because now that you see it clearly, you have a choice: **To move forward with wisdom, self-respect, and a heart free of regret.**

Healing starts with you. So let go of the guilt and shame and step into the future with a renewed self-love.

Because *you* deserve that.

THE POWER OF DIVINE TIMING

When you align yourself with purpose, wisdom, and discipline, opportunities will come to you—not by accident, but because you were ready for them.

Time is more than just hours and minutes ticking away it embodies **divine wisdom and alignment**. Everything happens at the right time, in the right way, and for the right reason. When you learn to trust the process and align yourself with divine timing, your success is already predetermined.

But here's the challenge: **You must stay in a place of readiness.**

Too often, people miss their moment not because they lack talent or opportunity but because they were unprepared when it arrived. Success isn't just about wanting something—it's about being in the right mindset and position to receive it.

Think about a farmer. They don't just hope for a good harvest; they prepare the soil, plant the seeds, and nurture the crops long before it's time to reap. The same applies to your life. You cannot expect a breakthrough if you have not been actively preparing for it.

Divine action follows divine alignment. When you align yourself with purpose, wisdom, and discipline, opportunities will come to you—not by accident, but because you were ready for them.

So, stay in a place of readiness. Develop your skills. Strengthen your mindset. Build your character. Because when the right door opens, you don't want to hesitate. You want to walk through it confidently, knowing you've done the work and are precisely where you are meant to be.

Trust the timing. Stay prepared. Your moment is coming.

BEYOND LACK: LIVING IN DIVINE PROVISION

Lack is not your identity. Just because you don't have something right now doesn't mean you never will.

It's easy to focus on what we don't have. The world constantly reminds us of our shortcomings what we should own, where we should be, and who we should have become by now. But here's the truth: **Don't let what you lack label you to the extent that it limits you.**

Lack is not your identity. Just because you don't have something *right now* doesn't mean you never will. Just because you're in a season of waiting doesn't mean you're in a lifetime of deficiency. The problem isn't what you lack it's how you *see* what you lack. If you allow it, scarcity can shrink your vision, make you doubt your worth, and keep you from moving forward. But lack is never meant to define you; it is meant to **refine** you.

Wherever you are right now, **life is still good**. Even if you don't have everything you want, look around—you still have breath in your lungs, strength in your body, and purpose in your soul. And most importantly, **God is making provision for you.**

Psalm 37:25 reminds us: *I have never seen the righteous forsaken or His seed begging bread.* This is not just a comforting phrase but a declaration of divine provision. You will not suffer lack. You will not beg. You will not go to bed hungry because **the Lord will supply all your needs according to His riches in glory**.

His riches are not limited by the economy, by your bank account, or by the circumstances around you. His provision does not depend on whether people approve of you, the opportunity looks promising, or whether you feel ready. **God provides in ways you don't even see yet.**

So, shift your mindset, stop looking at what's missing, and start focusing on what's promised. You are not forgotten, and you are not empty-handed. The provisions for your future are already in motion—you have to trust, prepare, and walk in faith.

You lack nothing. You are provided for. Now, live like it.

THE PITFALLS OF SMALL MINDS IN BIG POSITIONS

Power does not change people; it reveals them.

Authority is a powerful tool. When wielded correctly, it inspires, uplifts, and creates environments where people can thrive. But when placed in the wrong hands when given to someone unprepared, insecure, or power-hungry it becomes a weapon of destruction. The worst thing one can ever deal with is a small person in a prominent position.

Power does not change people; it reveals them. Small-minded people who suddenly find themselves in a leadership position do not grow into greatness. Instead, they become intoxicated by the authority, seeking to prove themselves through control rather than leadership. Instead of being a beacon of inspiration, they create a toxic work culture filled with fear, micromanagement, and inefficiency. Think about workplaces you've been in where bosses ruled through intimidation, insecurity, or favoritism. These leaders were not truly leading; they held positions they weren't prepared to handle. A small-minded person with power is more concerned with proving their superiority than building a team, and as a result, they suffocate creativity, growth, and morale.

The Explosion of Greatness Under Small Leadership

Greatness cannot thrive under small leadership for long. Conflict is inevitable when highly skilled, visionary, and hardworking individuals are under the authority of someone who lacks true leadership qualities. Greatness will always outgrow small-minded control, and when suppressed for too long, it erupts—sometimes in the form of employees leaving, rebellion against bad leadership, or a complete breakdown in productivity.

History has shown us that true leaders empower those around them, while weak leaders suppress others they fear will outshine them. A great leader understands their role is cultivating, mentoring, and elevating. A small leader, on the other hand, operates from a place of scarcity, feeling that any success outside of their own diminishes their value. For instance, a small leader might be a manager who constantly micromanages their team, while a great leader could be a CEO who encourages innovation and growth.

The Responsibility of True Leadership

If you ever find yourself in a position of authority, remember that your role is not to control but to guide. Authentic leadership is not about exercising power—it's about exercising wisdom. Here are three principles to ensure you remain a leader of integrity and impact:

Empower, Don't Overpower

Leadership is about lifting others up, not keeping them down. Recognize the strengths of those you lead and allow them to flourish.

Lead with Confidence, Not Insecurity

A strong leader is secure enough to welcome different perspectives, talents, and challenges. Insecurity breeds dictatorship; confidence breeds collaboration.

Stay Humble in Your Position

Authority is a privilege, not a right. The best leaders remember their origins and use their experiences to guide others rather than belittle them.

Overcoming the Small Leader

If you work under a small leader, the best approach is to remain professional, maintain integrity, and focus on growth. Toxic leadership will never sustain itself for long. Either the leader will change, or those under them will move on to more significant opportunities where their greatness is appreciated.

Ultimately, authentic leadership is not about titles, promotions, or power; it's about influence. Influence is something that a position cannot grant; it is earned through respect, character, and service. The world needs more leaders who understand authority is not about ruling over people but lifting them higher. Strive to be one of those leaders.

FEEL. DEAL. HEAL

Feel your truth, deal with your challenges, and heal into the fullest expression of your authentic self.

Allow yourself to feel exactly what you're dealing with right now even when it hurts. Too often, we try to disconnect from our emotions because we fear the pain they bring. Yet, when we shut off the signals coming from our body, those suppressed feelings find another way to express themselves often in ways that disrupt our peace and well-being.

Imagine your body as a finely tuned instrument. Every emotion, whether sorrow, anger, or joy, plays a vital role. When you ignore the natural cadence of these feelings, you risk the disharmony of unresolved emotions echoing in unexpected places. Instead, by sitting with your feelings and acknowledging them, you give yourself the gift of understanding and the chance to heal.

Take a moment to tune in: notice the sensations in your neck, the tension in your shoulders, the rhythm of your breath. These physical signals are your body's way of communicating what's happening within. Rather than disconnecting or numbing yourself to the discomfort, lean into it. Allow the sadness to surface, the frustration to build, and the pain to be present without judgment. This honest engagement is the first step toward transforming that energy into growth.

Remember, every emotion is a messenger. When you let yourself fully experience your feelings, you stop the cycle of disconnect and misdirected behaviour. The pain you feel now can be a powerful catalyst for change if you're willing to face it head-on. Embracing your emotions is not a sign of weakness; it's a courageous act of self-respect and self-care. It's a beacon of hope that leads to transformation.

Today, permit yourself to be human. Allow the storm of your emotions to pass through you, knowing that each drop of feeling is a chance to learn more about who you are and what you need. Trust that by honouring your authentic, physical experience, you will guide your life into a more authentic and balanced path. It's a journey towards self-acceptance and inner peace.

In that space of acceptance, you'll find the strength to move forward with clarity and compassion. Let your feelings be your guide, and remember: the more connected you are to your true self—from your neck down—the less likely those suppressed emotions will sneak up in harmful ways. Embrace your emotional truth, and watch how it transforms your inner world into a wellspring of resilience and growth.

Feel: Take a deep breath and invite every emotion to be present. Instead of numbing or avoiding the pain, lean into it. Every feeling you experience—sadness, anger, or even joy is a valuable messenger. By feeling full, you honour the truth of your inner world and pave the way for genuine self-understanding.

Deal: Once you have acknowledged your emotions, it's time to deal with them head-on. This means engaging with the challenges rather than pushing them aside. Break down your obstacles into manageable pieces and tackle them with courage and persistence. Remember, every challenge is an opportunity to learn, grow, and strengthen your resilience.

Heal: Healing comes naturally when you allow yourself the space to feel and the will to act. As you work through your emotions and confront your challenges, you create the conditions for proper healing. With time, compassion, and commitment to self-care, your scars can become symbols of strength and transformation.

EMBRACING THE FREEDOM TO CHANGE

It's important to remember that you have the right indeed, the freedom to change your mind.

Life is a journey of continuous evolution. We often set our sights on a dream, a profession, or a calling that ignites our passion. Yet, as time unfolds, we may discover that the path we once thought was our destiny no longer resonates with our deepest self. It's important to remember that you have the right—indeed, the freedom—to change your mind.

Our dreams are like stars: they guide, inspire, and light the way forward. But as we grow, our inner landscape shifts. What once seemed like the perfect constellation may begin to blur into something different. This transformation is not a sign of failure but a testament to your evolving identity. Each change of heart reflects deeper insights about who you are and what truly fulfills you. Embracing this evolution means honoring your present self rather than clinging to a past ideal.

Often, we enter into professions or ministries with a sense of purpose drawn by a vision of making a difference, achieving excellence, or living out our values. However, the reality of daily work can sometimes reveal that the dream isn't what we imagined. When the spark dims, listen carefully to that inner voice. It whispers the truth of your current needs and desires. You recognize that a shift might be necessary by tuning in—a sign that it's time to reimagine your path. This gentle and persistent inner guidance reminds you that your happiness and fulfillment are paramount.

Changing Course Is Not Giving Up

The common misconception is that changing your mind is akin to failure or indecision. In truth, it is an act of bravery. When you choose to pivot, you are not abandoning your dreams but refining them. Life experiences shape our understanding of what we truly want, and sometimes, that means moving away from a role or calling that no longer fits. Think of it as an artist reimagining their masterpiece. The willingness to change is a declaration of self-respect—a commitment to honoring your own growth rather than conforming to outdated expectations.

Every chapter of your life is written with the ink of possibility. You can rewrite your story when you recognize that your current path no longer serves your well-being or passion. This process might initially feel daunting, but it's also profoundly liberating. Embracing change allows you to explore uncharted territories where new opportunities await.

It's about permitting yourself to seek what brings genuine joy rather than staying on a path out of obligation or fear of the unknown.

Imagine the energy and excitement that accompany a fresh start. New challenges, new mentors, and new experiences can reignite your spirit. This new chapter isn't about erasing your past but building upon it. Every experience, even those that seem to have led you astray, has contributed to the person you are today. By integrating these lessons, you create a more authentic version of yourself, ready to pursue a path that aligns with your evolving passions.

Embracing Uncertainty with Optimism

Change is inherently uncertain, but that uncertainty is where potential lives. The unknown can be intimidating, yet it also brims with the possibility of discovering parts of yourself that have yet to bloom. Rather than fearing uncertainty, embrace it as a space of infinite opportunities. Each step into the unknown is a step towards growth. Trust that you have the resilience and insight to navigate new directions, even if the path isn't unclear.

Take a moment to reflect on past transitions. Recall the moments when stepping into the unfamiliar led to unexpected joy, new relationships, or renewed energy. These memories prove that change while challenging, is often the precursor to a richer, more fulfilling experience. By welcoming uncertainty with an open heart, you open yourself to the endless opportunities life offers.

Practical Steps to a New Beginning

Self-Reflection: Take time to evaluate your current situation. What aspects of your profession or ministry no longer fulfill you? What values and passions now call out for attention? Journaling, meditation, or conversations with trusted friends can illuminate your feelings.

Seek Inspiration: Look to stories of individuals who have reinvented themselves. Their journeys can offer valuable insights and affirm that change is a natural, positive part of life.

Set Clear Goals: Once you understand your new direction, set small, achievable goals leading to your vision. Each step forward builds confidence and momentum.

Build a Support System: Surround yourself with people who encourage and inspire you. Their support will be invaluable as you navigate this transition.

Embrace Learning: Consider new skills, courses, or mentorships that align with your revised goals. Lifelong learning can be a powerful catalyst for transformation.

Every decision to change course celebrates your growth and is a commitment to living authentically and boldly. Remember that the journey is just as important as the destination. Each twist and turn, every moment of doubt or exhilaration, is part of the mosaic that forms your unique story.

In a world that often prizes consistency over change, standing by your decision to evolve is a powerful act of self-love. It reminds you that you are more than your current title or role you are a dynamic, ever-changing individual with limitless potential.

THE PROCESS OF TRANSFORMATION: EMBRACING PAIN, PURPOSE, AND PROGRESS

The significance of your calling is far greater than the temporary suffering it may entail.

Life's journey is not always paved with certainty and clarity. Often, we find ourselves immersed in processes that seem to lack immediate purpose. Yet, it is precisely through these processes painful, challenging, and sometimes lonely that our true purpose is forged.

The Unseen Purpose in the Process

Sometimes, the steps you take may seem arbitrary or meaningless. The process can be murky, filled with setbacks and moments of doubt. However, every experience and hardship is essential to the intricate design that leads you to your destiny. You might not always see the purpose in the daily struggles but remember: you are being processed for a reason. Each trial and tribulation molds you, refining your spirit and preparing you for the life you are meant to lead.

The journey toward fulfilling your purpose is often marred by pain. The growth process is rarely comfortable, marked by sacrifices, moments of isolation, and the inevitable feeling of being overwhelmed. But consider this:

your pain is not a punishment nor a dead end. It is a necessary catalyst for growth. Like a sculptor chiseling away at a block of marble, the challenges you face are carving out the masterpiece that is your life.

When the path is steep and the destination is shrouded in uncertainty, it is vital to remain steadfast. The process may demand persistence and unwavering faith. Stick to your plan—trust in the journey, even when progress seems slow. Your perseverance is not just about enduring hardship but actively engaging with each life lesson. Every setback is a setup for a more significant comeback, reinforcing that your struggles are integral to your evolution.

Purpose Over Pain: The Ultimate Declaration

Your purpose transcends the fleeting moments of pain you encounter. It is a beacon that shines through the darkest of times, reminding you that every hardship has its place in the grand tapestry of your life. The significance of your calling is far greater than the temporary suffering it may entail. Embrace this truth with conviction: You are destined to fulfill a purpose uniquely yours, and nothing—not even the most agonizing challenges—can stand in the way of that destiny.

So, you will not cease to exist until your purpose is fully realized. This is not merely an optimistic platitude but a powerful affirmation of the resilience and potential that lies within you. Your journey is not defined by the pain of its process but by the strength and wisdom you gain.

Moving Forward with Conviction

As you navigate the twists and turns of your path, hold onto this guiding principle: every moment of struggle is a step toward a deeper, more profound destiny. Embrace the process with gratitude for the lessons it brings, and trust that every difficulty is an essential part of your transformation. Your purpose is not a destination that is reached—it is the very journey of becoming, of evolving into the best version of yourself.

As you face challenges head-on each day, remember that the process, as arduous as it may be, is a necessary rite of passage. The growth you experience is the foundation upon which your extraordinary future is built. Let your pain fuel your passion, and let your persistence be the bridge that carries you to a life of fulfillment and meaning.

Your journey is unique, and your purpose is monumental. Stand firm in your resolve, knowing that every trial you endure is a testament to your strength. The process is your teacher, and through it, you will unlock your limitless potential.

EMBRACING YOUR AUTHENTIC JOURNEY

Embrace your individuality, nurture your passions, and commit to continuous growth.

In a world that often celebrates conformity, the greatest act of courage is to follow your own unique path. It's all too common to find ourselves chasing after another person's approval, attention, or love, hoping they'll validate our worth. But when we do this, we lose sight of our passions, potential for growth, and dreams. Instead of bending ourselves to fit someone else's expectations, imagine the power of pursuing what sets your soul on fire and building a world that reflects the real you.

Many of us have experienced the bittersweet feeling of trying to gain acceptance or love from someone who seems to have it all figured out. We start comparing our lives to theirs, often feeling inadequate or as if we're perpetually on the outside looking in. This chase can be exhausting, an endless pursuit that diverts precious energy from developing our true selves.

Chasing another person is not just about seeking external validation; it's also about surrendering the responsibility for your own happiness. When your joy depends on someone else's acknowledgement, you give away control of your destiny. Instead, consider what might happen if you redirected that energy inward. What if you focused on nurturing your interests, talents, and ambitions? You'd be taking the first step towards a life that isn't defined by the fleeting opinions of others.

Discovering Your Passions

Every person is born with unique talents and interests, even if they're sometimes hidden under layers of self-doubt and societal expectations. Finding your passion is like discovering a hidden treasure within yourself. It might be art, music, technology, writing, or a cause close to your heart. When you allow yourself to explore these passions, you invest in personal growth and happiness.

Pursuing your passions isn't always easy. It requires stepping out of your comfort zone, often facing challenges and setbacks. But each struggle is a stepping stone, each setback a lesson, and each small victory a reminder that you are indeed on your path. Whenever you choose passion over validation, you reclaim your power and move closer to a life filled with purpose and fulfillment.

Growing Through Self-Improvement

Self-improvement is a lifelong journey a commitment to becoming the best version of yourself. Instead of conforming to someone else's standards or proving that you belong, focus on improving yourself daily. This might mean learning new skills, expanding your knowledge, or developing habits that nurture your well-being.

Growth is an internal process. It's about setting your own benchmarks and celebrating every milestone, no matter how small. When you invest in yourself, you create a solid foundation for lasting happiness and success. Personal growth also means embracing your imperfections. Understand that mistakes and failures are not signs of weakness but opportunities for learning and transformation. With every challenge you overcome, you build resilience and confidence qualities that will serve you well in every aspect of your life.

Building Your Own World

Imagine a world built entirely on your terms, reflecting your values, dreams, and passions. Rather than trying to fit into a mold created by someone else, why not make your own? Building your own world is an empowering act of self-expression. It means designing a life where your priorities and dreams take center stage.

Creating this world starts with self-awareness. Reflect on what truly matters to you. What are the values that you hold dear? What dreams keep you awake at night, filling you with excitement? Once you have a clear vision, take small, deliberate steps toward that future. This might involve setting personal goals, cultivating a supportive community, or changing your surroundings to align with your vision better. Every choice you make is a brick in the foundation of your personal world a world where you are not trying to earn someone else's love or approval but rather celebrating your unique person.

One of the most challenging aspects of following your own path is the fear of loneliness. It can feel intimidating to stand alone when the norm is to seek companionship and validation from others. However, true strength lies in the courage to stand by yourself. Being comfortable in your skin means you don't need to seek validation from the outside world constantly.

By focusing on your growth and dreams, you become less dependent on external influences. This independence allows you to develop a deeper, more genuine connection with yourself. And when you love and accept who you are, you naturally attract people and opportunities that resonate with your true self. Instead of feeling isolated, you'll find that you are surrounded by those who appreciate you for who you are, not for an image you're trying to uphold.

Celebrating Your Unique Path

Every step you take towards building your own world is a victory worth celebrating. The journey may be filled with uncertainties and challenges but rich with possibilities and personal triumphs. As you commit to chasing your passions, fostering growth, and pursuing your dreams, you create your life authentically and unapologetically.

Remember, the most rewarding achievements often come from the courage to be different. It's in the moments when you follow your heart rather than the crowd that you truly shine. So, dare to be different. Embrace your journey with all its twists and turns. Let every day be an opportunity to create a life that reflects your true passions and dreams.

Don't waste another moment chasing after someone else's version of success or trying to prove that you belong in their world. The energy you spend on that chase could be invested in building a future where you are the architect of your own happiness. Embrace your individuality, nurture your passions, and commit to continuous growth. In doing so, you will discover a profound sense of fulfillment and a life that is not only successful but also deeply meaningful.

Your journey is uniquely yours, and every step you take toward building your world is a testament to the incredible strength and potential that resides within you. Take that step, and let your true self light the way forward.

THE WORK IN THE SHADOWS

True success isn't about what you do when the world is watching it's about the work you put in when no one is around to applaud you.

Success is never an accident. It results from relentless effort, unseen sacrifices, and countless hours of dedication when no one is watching. The world often celebrates the final product—an artist unveiling a masterpiece, an athlete lifting a trophy, an entrepreneur launching a successful business but people don't see the endless nights of struggle, failures, doubts, and unwavering commitment behind the scenes. The truth is that the work done in solitude, when no audience is present, is the foundation upon which all greatness is built.

In a world that thrives on instant gratification, it's easy to feel discouraged when results don't come quickly. You might spend months or even years refining your craft, building your skills, or pushing your limits without recognition. You may wonder if all the effort is worth it, if anyone will ever notice the work you've poured your heart into. But that's the defining difference between those who succeed and those who don't—successful people trust the process. They know that every extra hour spent practicing, every moment of discipline, and every failure turned into a lesson shapes them into someone unstoppable.

Imagine an athlete training before sunrise while the rest of the world sleeps, a writer crafting stories long before they find an audience, or a musician playing in an empty room, perfecting each note. These moments of isolation might feel insignificant at the time, but they are the ones that matter most. The person who dedicates themselves fully when no one is watching will one day command the attention of many. When the moment of opportunity arrives, those prepared in silence will be ready to shine.

The difference between those who make an impact and those who fade into obscurity is persistence. Many people start strong, motivated by initial excitement or external validation, but when that validation disappears, so does their effort. The ones who rise above are those who continue even when the applause is absent. They understand that genuine commitment isn't fueled by recognition but by an internal drive to be better than they were yesterday.

If you find yourself in the grind, feeling unnoticed and unappreciated, remember this: the world may not see you yet, but it will. Every great success story begins in the dark, where no one is watching, where only the individual knows the depth of their sacrifice. But when the time is right, when preparation meets opportunity, the world will take notice. And by then, you won't just be ready—you'll be unstoppable.

THE POWER OF PURPOSE OVER POPULARITY

Deliverance will be birthed not because of human approval, but because of divine authority.

True deliverance isn't about approval it's about assignment. It's easy to believe that breakthrough is tied to how others perceive us, but purpose isn't dependent on popularity. Whether people like you or not, whether they agree with you or not, your mission remains the same. You weren't called to fit in you were called to disrupt, to break chains, and to shift atmospheres.

There is an undeniable battle over every life, a war in the unseen realms. Cycles of oppression, generational curses, and demonic assignments seek to keep people bound, repeating the same struggles as those who came before them. But when God gives an assignment, it isn't for comfort—it's for confrontation. Your presence, prayers, and obedience are all weapons in the spirit, tearing down strongholds and manifesting deliverance.

Some will resist you. Some will misunderstand you. Some may even reject you. But that doesn't change your calling. Jesus Himself was despised and rejected, yet He never wavered. He didn't need the approval to fulfil His purpose.

Likewise, you are not here to be liked but to set captives free. When you walk in your divine assignment, you carry an authority that disrupts the enemy's plans. You are a breaker, an interrupter of darkness, and a vessel of God's power.

Deliverance is often uncomfortable. It requires disrupting cycles that people have learned to live with. It challenges mindsets, exposes hidden chains, and demands change. But freedom is always worth the fight. Your presence, your prayers, and your unwavering obedience to God's call will shift the atmosphere and dismantle every demonic pattern holding people hostage.

So don't be discouraged when you face resistance. Don't shrink back when people don't like the truth you carry. Your assignment is more significant than their approval. Keep pressing forward, speaking life, and disrupting the enemy's plans. Because when God sends a deliverer, no demon, no generational curse, and no opposition can stand in the way. Deliverance will be birthed—not because of human approval, but because of divine authority.

And that authority is yours. Walk in it.

THE HEALING BEFORE THE MESSAGE

To truly impact lives, we must first allow ourselves to be healed.

Words have power. They can build or break, heal or harm, inspire or injure. But we often speak from a place of pain rather than peace. When our hearts carry unhealed wounds, our words reflect them—sometimes harshly, sometimes defensively, and sometimes in ways that push people further away instead of drawing them toward transformation.

It is a sobering reality that our truth, as we perceive it, is often incomplete. Our experiences, past hurts, and personal biases filter the way we see the world and, in turn, the way we communicate. An unattended wound will always be known through anger, sarcasm, defensiveness, or even silence. And when we speak from that place of unresolved pain, our words may carry more judgment than wisdom, emotion than intention, and bitterness than grace.

But truth, at its core, is not just about being right it's about bringing light. And light is best received when it is given with love, clarity, and compassion. If we aim to help others grow and challenge them toward something more significant, we must first examine our hearts. Are we speaking to heal or to hurt? Are we driven by love or by our own need for validation? Are we more concerned with proving a point or making a difference?

Healing does not mean ignoring the truth or watering it down. It means delivering it in a way that makes it easier to hear, understand, and receive. The most potent messages don't come from wounded souls—they come from whole hearts. Wholeness brings wisdom. Clarity brings kindness. Healing brings the ability to see beyond ourselves and consider the weight of our words on another person's heart. To truly impact lives, we must first allow ourselves to be healed. Healing requires humility, self-awareness, and the willingness to confront our wounds before addressing others. When we do this, we shift from speaking *at* people to speaking *to* them. Our words become bridges instead of barriers, tools of transformation instead of weapons of destruction.

So, before you speak, ask yourself: *Am I speaking from a place of love or pain?*

The difference between speaking from love and speaking from pain isn't always apparent at the moment, but here are some ways to discern the source of your words:

Signs You're Speaking from Pain:
- Your words carry a sharp edge more judgment than guidance.
- You feel a strong emotional charge (anger, resentment, frustration) while speaking.
- Your goal is to be heard, not necessarily to help.
- You feel the need to defend, justify, or prove something.
- Your words come from a personal wound rather than a genuine concern for others.

Signs You're Speaking from Love:
- Your words aim to uplift, even when they challenge.
- You pause and consider how the other person might receive your message.
- Your intention is clarity and healing, not just venting frustration.
- You speak with patience, even when addressing hard truths.
- You feel peace after speaking rather than regret or further agitation.

If you're unsure, take a step back. Ask yourself: *What do I truly want this person to walk away with? Am I trying to heal or unload?* The goal should always be connection, growth, and understanding. When we lead with love, even brutal truths become more straightforward.

Let your words be filled with both truth and grace. Let them be a light that guides, not a fire that burns. And above all, let your healing be the foundation for the wisdom you share because only then will your message truly change lives.

THE POWER OF LETTING GO

Not everyone is meant to go where you're going. Some people will stay behind, content in their comfort zones, unwilling to stretch beyond their limitations.

One of the most challenging life lessons is realising that you can't make people change. No matter how much you pour into them or how deeply you believe in their potential, some people won't grow. Not because they can't but because they won't. Growth requires a willingness to evolve, to confront hard truths, and to put in the necessary work. And the truth is, not everyone is willing to take that journey.

It's natural to want the best for those around us. We see their possibilities, untapped greatness, and the lives they could live if they embraced change. But when someone refuses to take responsibility for their growth, you cannot carry them. You cannot drag them toward a future they refuse to claim for themselves. Growth is not something you can force it must be chosen.

There comes a time when you must accept that your desire for someone's breakthrough cannot exceed their own. You can inspire, encourage, and offer wisdom but cannot do the work for them. If they resist, stay stuck in old patterns, and refuse to be complicit in their transformation, then you have to decide: Do you keep exhausting yourself trying to lift someone who won't move, or do you release them and continue on your path?

Letting go is not an act of cruelty it is an act of wisdom. Holding on to people who refuse to grow will only drain, frustrate, and slow your progress. It doesn't mean you don't love them. It doesn't mean you've given up on them. It means you recognize that you cannot carry someone who won't walk.

True leaders, mentors, and visionaries understand this: You can only help those willing to help themselves. You can plant the seed but not force it to grow. You can extend a hand, but they must choose to take it. And if they won't, you must be strong enough to move forward without them.

Not everyone is meant to go where you're going. Some people will stay behind, content in their comfort zones, unwilling to stretch beyond their limitations. And that's okay. Your job is not to carry them it's to keep moving and growing and to surround yourself with those ready to walk in the same direction.

So, release the weight. Let go of what is holding you back. Love and pray for them, but don't lose yourself trying to change someone who doesn't want to. The journey ahead is too incredible, and your purpose is too essential to be slowed down by those who refuse to grow. Keep moving forward, and trust that those who are meant to walk with you will rise to meet you on the path.

BEYOND YOUR CIRCUMSTANCES

You are more than your missed opportunities, more tha n your failures, and more than your setbacks.

You are more than your circumstances. More than the doors that have been closed to you. More than the opportunities that never came. Too often, people define their potential by what is currently available, assuming that if the path isn't clear, the dream must not be possible. But real greatness is not measured by the opportunities handed to you it is measured by your ability to keep pushing forward, even when the odds seem stacked against you.

Life has a way of making dreams feel impossible. You may have tried and failed. You may have faced rejection, lack of support, or unforeseen setbacks that made your vision feel out of reach. But just because something is broken doesn't mean it's beyond repair. Sometimes, the most powerful dreams are the ones that survive the storm, the ones you refuse to let go of, even when the world tells you to move on.

Do not let temporary obstacles become permanent limitations. If the opportunity you need doesn't exist, create one. If the door is closed, build your entrance. Some of the greatest success stories in history were birthed from people who refused to be defined by their lack of resources. They chose to see beyond their limitations and believed in something more significant. And that same resilience lives in you.

Your dreams are still valid, no matter how broken they may seem. You are not limited by what is in front of you—you are only limited by what you believe about yourself. Keep learning, keep preparing, and keep believing. Even if it takes longer than expected and the journey looks different than you imagined, your dream still has the power to become a reality.

So, refuse to settle. Refuse to give up. You are more than your missed opportunities, more than your failures, and more than your setbacks. You are capable of rising above it all. Keep moving forward, and one day, the world will see what you've known all along—your dream was never broken, only waiting for the right moment to be fulfilled.

THE POWER OF SELF-RESPECT

People who benefit from your silence will always be uncomfortable with your strength.

Standing up for yourself is not a flaw. It is not an act of rebellion nor an invitation for conflict. It is a declaration of self-worth. Yet, too often, people are made to feel guilty for asserting themselves, as if valuing their feelings, needs, and boundaries is an inconvenience to others. But here's the truth: You have every right to speak up. You have every right to express your emotions. And you have every right to say *No* without guilt.

Society often praises self-sacrifice, primarily when it benefits others. It makes people believe that silence is maturity, that agreeing is easier than disrupting the peace, and that saying *no is selfish. But real peace—true, lasting, soul-deep—does* not come from suppressing yourself to keep others comfortable. It comes from honouring your voice, even when others don't want to hear it.

If someone makes you feel like standing up for yourself is "too much," that's a reflection of *them*, not you. People who benefit from your silence will always be uncomfortable with your strength. Those who only respect you when you are agreeable do not truly respect you. And if someone dismisses your feelings, ignores your needs, or constantly crosses your boundaries, they show you who they are. Believe them.

Re-evaluating your circle is not an act of disloyalty—it is an act of self-preservation. You were not placed on this earth to shrink yourself for the comfort of others. The people in your life should uplift you, respect you, and value your presence, not manipulate, belittle, or guilt you into compliance. Surround yourself with those who celebrate your voice, not those who silence it.

Let go of the fear of being misunderstood. You are not too much. You are not selfish. You are not oversensitive. You are simply a person who understands their worth and that is something you should never apologise for. Stand firm, speak boldly, and walk in the confidence that those who truly belong in your life will respect and honour the person you are becoming.

THE COST OF COMPROMISE

The actual test of character is not in moments of comfort but in moments of challenge.

At the moment, compromise can feel like a relief. It can seem like the easiest path, the most convenient option, or even a necessary sacrifice. But what feels satisfying today can become a source of deep regret tomorrow, especially at the expense of our morals, values, and standards.

Life will always present opportunities to take shortcuts, to bend the truth, or to lower our standards for temporary gain. It might be easier to stay silent when you should speak up, to accept less than you deserve rather than risk rejection, or to follow the crowd rather than stand alone. In those moments, compromise seems small and insignificant even. But small compromises add up, and before you know it, you've drifted far from who you once were.

Regret rarely comes instantly. It comes later when the weight of our choices settles in. It comes when we realize we sacrificed long-term peace for short-term pleasure. When we recognize that we traded integrity for approval, authenticity for acceptance, or purpose for convenience, what once felt like an easy decision can become what keeps us up at night.

The true test of character is not in moments of comfort but in moments of challenge. When everything in you wants to take the easy road, will you stand firm? When the pressure to conform is heavy, will you hold onto your values? When temptation whispers that no one will know, will you remember that *you* will know? Because in the end, we do not answer to the opinions of others—we answer to our conscience and God.

Short-term satisfaction is never worth long-term regret. Every choice you make is a step in one direction or another. Are you walking toward the life you truly desire, or are you taking detours that will leave you lost? When faced with the temptation to compromise, ask yourself: *Will I be proud of this decision tomorrow? Will my future self thank me or resent me?*

Your values are your foundation. Protect them. Your morals are your compass. Follow them. Your standards are your boundaries. Uphold them. Because the most remarkable success is not found in what you gain but in who you become. And when you refuse to compromise what truly matters, you will build a life that is not just successful but honorable, fulfilling, and free of regret.

BUILD YOUR OWN WORLD

You were meant to be in pursuit of purpose.

Too often, we spend our energy chasing people seeking validation, love, or approval from those who may never fully see our worth. We bend, shrink, and compromise to fit into someone else's world, hoping they will choose us, accept us, or recognize our value. But in pursuing someone else, we often lose sight of ourselves.

The truth is, no one should have to be convinced to see your worth. The right people will recognize it effortlessly. You're chasing the wrong thing if you constantly prove that you belong in someone's life. Instead of chasing people, chase your passions. Instead of seeking to fit into their world, build your own.

When you invest in yourself—your dreams, growth, and purpose—you naturally attract those who align with your journey. Confidence, success, and fulfillment come from within, not external validation. When you focus on becoming the best version of yourself, the right people will gravitate toward you—not because you chased them, but because you became someone worth knowing, worth respecting, and worth loving.

Your energy is precious. Why waste it running after people who may never truly appreciate you? Pour that energy into your ambitions, craft, and personal evolution. The more you grow, the clearer who is meant to walk with you. Those who belong in your life will not require chasing; they will walk alongside you willingly, inspired by your journey rather than needing to be convinced of your value.

So, stop seeking a seat at someone else's table. Build your own. Design a life so meaningful and purpose-driven that people don't just notice you—they *respect* you. When you create a world that reflects your dreams, values, and purpose, the right people will not just enter it; they will cherish the opportunity to be part of it.

You were never meant to be in pursuit of others. You were meant to be in pursuit of purpose. Chase *that*—and everything meant for you will follow.

TALENT OPENS DOORS, AND DISCIPLINE KEEPS THEM OPEN

The most successful individuals are not necessarily the most talented but the most disciplined.

Talent is a gift, but discipline is a choice. Many people are born with extraordinary abilities—athletes who can move with effortless precision, musicians who can create magic with a single note, and speakers who can captivate an entire room. But talent alone is never enough. It can open doors, create opportunities, and even bring temporary success, but without discipline, that success will not last.

The world is filled with talented people who never reach their full potential. Why? Because they rely on their natural abilities without putting in the work to refine them. Talent may be noticed, but discipline determines whether you stay in the game. Discipline is waking up early to train, even when no one is watching. It's studying when others are relaxing, practising when you don't feel like it, and committing to constant growth even when you've already achieved success.

Discipline is what separates the great from the good. Many people have potential, but only a few are willing to push beyond comfort to maximize it. The most successful individuals are not necessarily the most talented but the most disciplined. They show up, put in the effort, and remain consistent, even when motivation fades.

Think of a door. Your talent is the key—it can unlock opportunities and open new paths. But what happens once you step through? If you lack discipline, the door that once swung wide open will eventually close. Without discipline, you become stagnant, relying on past achievements instead of building new ones. But if you are willing to put in the work and commit to excellence day after day, your success will not only continue it will multiply.

So, don't let your talent be wasted. Sharpen it, develop it, and back it up with relentless discipline. Show up when it's hard. Push through when it's uncomfortable. Refuse to settle for being merely "gifted" when you have the potential to be great. Ultimately, talent may get you in the room, but discipline will determine whether you stay and thrive.

EMBRACING THE LIMITLESS NATURE OF GOD

To define God is to confine Him
within the walls of our human logic,
and yet, He transcends every thought, every concept, and every idea
we could ever formulate.

The minute you start to define God, you limit Him. No matter how rich, human language remains inadequate to fully encapsulate God's greatness. Our words fall short, our descriptions remain incomplete, and our understanding is only a fraction of the vastness of His being. To define God is to confine Him within the walls of our human logic, and yet, He transcends every thought, every concept, and every idea we could ever formulate.

The constraints of human perception do not bind God's character. He is beyond what we can articulate, beyond what we can comprehend, and certainly beyond what we can predict. His ways are higher, His love is more profound, and His power is more significant than anything our finite minds can grasp. When we try to fit God into a neat, understandable box, we diminish the reality of who He truly is—Limitless.

A God Who Does More Than We Imagine

If God can DO above all that we can ask or think, how much more does His very nature exceed our ability to define? Ephesians 3:20 reminds us that He can do "exceedingly abundantly above all that we ask or think." This means that even our biggest dreams, highest hopes, and deepest desires are still small compared to what God is capable of accomplishing. If His works are beyond our imagination, how much more is His CHARACTER beyond our comprehension?

This truth should be a source of motivation and encouragement. When life presents obstacles, fear creeps in, or doubts cloud our faith, we must remember that our thoughts, circumstances, or abilities do not limit God. He is boundless in power, infinite in wisdom, and eternal in love. Nothing is too complicated for Him, no challenge too great, and no problem too complex. The natural world does not restrain him—He operates in the supernatural.

Living with a Limitless Perspective

Understanding that God is limitless should transform the way we live. It should shift our perspective from one of limitation to one of possibility. We often approach life with fears, thinking our problems are insurmountable, or our dreams are unattainable. But when we acknowledge that God is more significant than our limitations, we walk in faith, not fear. We stop relying on our strength and start trusting in His boundless power.

This should also impact how we pray. Instead of small, timid prayers, we should pray bold, faith-filled prayers, knowing that God can do far more than we can even conceive. Instead of living in doubt, we should walk confidently because our trust is not in ourselves but in a God with no limits.

Whatever you are facing, God is more prominent. Whatever you are dreaming, God's plans are greater. Whatever you are hoping for, His ability to provide surpasses your imagination. He is not a God confined by time, space, or human understanding—He is the Almighty, the Creator, the Uncontainable, the Limitless One.

You serve a God whom human words cannot define because He is beyond them. Trust in His limitless power, rest in His boundless love and live in the freedom that comes from knowing He is infinitely more than you can ever imagine.

STRENGTH BEYOND THE BREAKING POINT

*Strength is not just about endurance;
it's about transformation.*

True strength is not measured by how much weight you can carry before you crumble—it is measured by your ability to rise even after you have been broken. Life has a way of testing you, pushing you to the edge, and stretching you beyond what you ever thought you could bear. And when you think you can't take any more, life will demand more from you.

You will never know how strong you are until being strong is your only option. It's easy to talk about resilience when life is smooth, but true strength is revealed in the moments that challenge you to your core. It's in the nights when you cry but still wake up the next morning ready to fight. It's in the days when everything inside you wants to quit, but you take one more step forward. It's in the moments when you feel shattered, yet somehow, you gather the broken pieces and rebuild.

Being broken does not mean you are weak. Some of the strongest people have experienced the most profound pain but refused to let it define them. They have faced betrayal, loss, failure, and disappointment, but instead of giving up, they used those experiences as fuel to rise stronger. They allowed their hardships to shape them, not shatter them.

Strength is not just about endurance; it's about transformation. The breaking may feel unbearable, but it is often the birthplace of growth. Just as gold is refined by fire, your struggles refine you, making you wiser, bolder, and more resilient. Every challenge you face prepares you for what is coming next. Every hardship strengthens the foundation of the person you are becoming.

So, if you are in a season where life feels unbearable or like you've been broken beyond repair, know this: You are stronger than you think. This moment will not break you; it will build you. And one day, you will look back and realize that the very thing you thought would destroy you was the thing that made you unstoppable.

CULTIVATING A HABIT OF EXCELLENCE

Excellence must be your standard.

Excellence is not an innate trait bestowed upon a select few; it is a deliberate practice, a habit cultivated through consistent effort and unwavering commitment. Striving for excellence means pursuing the best version of oneself in every endeavor, transforming ordinary actions into extraordinary achievements.

Setting Clear and Ambitious Goals

The journey toward excellence begins with a clear vision. Define what success looks like in your personal and professional life. Establish specific, measurable, and challenging goals that align with your passions and values. Breaking these objectives into actionable steps creates a roadmap, guiding your daily efforts and providing a sense of direction. Regularly reviewing and adjusting your goals ensures they remain relevant and reflect your evolving aspirations.

Central to pursuing excellence is the belief that dedication and hard work can develop abilities and intelligence. This growth mindset transforms challenges into opportunities for learning and growth. Embrace failures as valuable lessons, understanding that setbacks are not reflections of your worth but stepping stones toward mastery. Viewing obstacles as opportunities builds resilience and fosters a continuous drive toward self-improvement.

Excellence is achieved through deliberate practice, and engaging in activities specifically designed to improve performance. Focus on areas that require development, set high standards, and seek feedback to refine your skills. This intentional and focused effort, repeated consistently, transforms actions into habits, leading to mastery and exceptional performance.

A commitment to lifelong learning fuels the pursuit of excellence. Cultivate an insatiable curiosity by seeking knowledge from diverse sources, attending workshops, reading extensively, and engaging in meaningful conversations. Expanding your horizons fosters innovation, adaptability, and a deeper understanding of the world around you.

Discipline is the backbone of excellence. Establish routines that prioritise your goals and adhere to them diligently. Even on challenging days, uphold your commitments, recognising that consistency in effort leads to significant achievements over time. Maintaining discipline builds a strong foundation upon which excellence is constructed.

Surrounding yourself with individuals who inspire, challenge, and support you is crucial in the journey toward excellence. Mentors, peers, and loved ones provide valuable perspectives, encouragement, and accountability. Engaging with a community that shares your commitment to growth enriches your experience and amplifies your development.

The path to excellence is dynamic and ever-evolving. Be open to change and willing to adapt your strategies as needed. Flexibility allows you to navigate obstacles, seize new opportunities, and continuously align your actions with your goals. By embracing adaptability, you remain resilient in the face of challenges and responsive to the demands of an ever-changing environment.

Prioritising Balance and Well-Being

Sustainable excellence thrives on a foundation of well-being. Prioritise physical health through regular exercise, sufficient rest, and a balanced diet. Nurture your mental and emotional health by engaging in activities that bring joy, practising mindfulness, and setting boundaries to prevent burnout. Maintaining balance ensures that your pursuit of excellence is fulfilling and enduring.

Incorporating these principles into your daily life transforms the pursuit of excellence from a lofty ideal into a lived reality. Each step taken with intention and dedication brings you closer to your fullest potential, turning the habit of excellence into a way of life.

WHEN WORK BECOMES PURPOSE

Purpose-driven work is not about chasing money, status, or titles it's about aligning your skills, passions, and values with something that matters.

Work is often seen as something we *must do—a responsibility, obligation, and* means to an end. But what if work wasn't just about making a living? What if it was about making a difference? What if, instead of something we dread, work becomes something that ignites our passion, fuels our spirit, and gives our lives deeper meaning?

When you wake up excited about what you do every morning, work ceases to feel like a burden. It becomes a calling, a purpose, an extension of who you are. The hours no longer feel like they are being *spent* but instead *invested*. You stop counting the minutes until the day ends because you are too engrossed in the joy of creation, service, and impact.

Purpose-driven work is not about chasing money, status, or titles—it's about aligning your skills, passions, and values with something that matters. It's about knowing that what you do contributes to a bigger picture. It doesn't mean every day will be easy or challenges won't arise. But when your work is rooted in purpose, even the struggles become meaningful. The setbacks become lessons. The effort feels worth it.

The key is to discover what fuels your spirit. What excites you? What problems do you feel called to solve? What work makes you feel alive rather than drained? When you align your work with your purpose, motivation comes naturally. You no longer need to force yourself to wake up early or push through exhaustion because your drive comes from within.

Imagine a life where Mondays don't feel like a curse but a new opportunity. A life where your work leaves a legacy, your impact stretches beyond a paycheck, and your career isn't just a job but a journey of growth and fulfillment. That life is possible—but it requires you to choose passion over complacency, purpose over routine, and meaning over mediocrity.

So, don't just work for survival—work for significance. Chase the kind of work that sets your soul on fire, makes you excited to wake up, and turns effort into joy. Because when you do what you were created to do, work stops feeling like work, and life becomes an extraordinary adventure.

RISE AGAIN: THE POWER OF PERSEVERANCE

In life, you will have ups and downs.
But don't allow your downs to keep you down.

Life is a journey filled with highs and lows, victories and setbacks. No one is exempt from hardship. Whether it's the weight of personal loss, failure, or unexpected challenges, we all face moments that threaten to keep us down. But the accurate measure of a person is not found in how they handle the mountaintop moments — it is revealed in how they rise after falling.

In life, you will have ups and downs. But don't allow your downs to keep you down. Dig deep in your inner being for that willpower and perseverance to conquer. Then get up and keep moving.

Falling is inevitable. At some point, life will knock you off your feet. It may be the loss of a loved one, the collapse of a dream, or the betrayal of someone you trusted. These moments can be crushing, leaving you breathless and unsure how to move forward. It's tempting to stay down — to wallow in self-pity, doubt, or fear. The weight of disappointment can make it feel impossible to get back up.

But here's the truth: falling isn't what defines you. Staying down does.

When life pushes you to the ground, you have two choices: stay there or rise. Rising isn't always easy, but it is always possible. The key lies in tapping into the strength that resides deep within you. Even in your darkest moments, a flicker of willpower is waiting to be reignited.

Dig deep. Find that inner spark of resilience. Remind yourself of the times you've overcome adversity before. You are stronger than you realize. The human spirit is remarkably resilient, capable of enduring more than we often believe. Trust that there is a well of strength inside you, waiting to be drawn upon.

Perseverance: The Bridge to Victory

Perseverance is not about ignoring pain — it's about pushing through it. It's the decision to keep going, even when the odds are stacked against you. Each step forward, no matter how small, is a victory. Every moment you choose to rise, you build a stronger, wiser, and more resilient version of yourself.

Even the most successful people have faced failure. The difference is that they didn't allow their setbacks to define them. They dug deep, found the courage to keep moving, and eventually reached new heights.

Movement is healing. You create momentum when you refuse to stay down and take even the smallest step forward. That momentum grows with each decision to rise. Action breeds confidence. Progress, no matter how slow, is still progress. The key is to keep moving — one step, one breath, one moment at a time.

You may stumble. You may even fall again. But as long as you keep rising, you are winning. Life's most significant victories belong to those who refuse to stay down.

A Call to Rise

So, when life knocks you down — and it will — remember this: **You are not defeated unless you choose to stay down. Dig deep, find your strength, and rise. Keep moving. Your next victory is waiting on the other side of perseverance.**

In every fall, there is an invitation to rise again. Accept it. Stand tall. Keep pushing forward. The world needs the strength that lies within you.

THE POWER OF THOUGHT: SHAPING YOUR REALITY

The expectation of thought influences behavior.

Your mind is the most powerful tool you possess. It can shape your perception, guide your actions, and ultimately determine the course of your life. Whether you realize it or not, the expectation of thought influences behavior. **As a man or woman thinks, so is he or she.** This truth is woven into the fabric of our existence, and nowhere is it more evident than in the phenomenon known as the placebo effect.

The Placebo Effect: Proof of Mind Over Matter

The placebo effect remarkably demonstrates the mind's influence over the body. In medicine, a patient may be given a sugar pill, told it's a powerful drug, and begin to experience healing — not because of the pill itself, but because they *believed* it would work. Their expectation triggered a physical response. The body responded to the mind's belief.

But what if this isn't limited to medicine? What if the same principle applies to your life?

Maybe you are where you are today because of what you think of yourself. If deep down you believe you don't deserve better — whether it's success, love, or happiness — your actions will align with that belief. You might not take risks. You might settle for less. You might sabotage opportunities without even realizing it.

The mind sends subtle messages that shape your environment. If you constantly tell yourself that you're not smart, talented, or worthy enough, the world around you will begin to reflect that narrative. Doors won't open because you won't knock. Opportunities will pass because you won't reach them. Your life becomes a mirror of your thoughts.

Your emotions are also shaped by the messages your mind is sending. If you believe the world is against you, you'll respond defensively. Maybe you're angry because you expect disappointment. Maybe you're bitter because you've convinced yourself that life is unfair and stacked against you. The mind plants seeds, and your behaviour waters them. Before you know it, you're acting out a story you subconsciously wrote. The world is responding not to who you *are* but to who you *think* you are.

Changing the Narrative

The good news is this: just as negative thoughts can hold you back, positive thoughts can propel you forward. You have the power to rewrite the script. Start by challenging the negative narratives that play on repeat in your mind.

Ask yourself:
- *What do I truly believe about myself?*
- *Are these beliefs serving me or limiting me?*
- *What would happen if I believed I deserved more?*

When you change your thoughts, you change your behavior. When you change your behavior, you change your life. The mind may not be able to control everything, but it can influence more than we realize.

A New Expectation

The placebo effect teaches us that belief can alter reality. What if you believed in your potential? What if you expected good things instead of fearing the worst? What if you trained your mind to see possibilities instead of limitations?

You don't have to be a victim of circumstance. You can shape your environment by shifting your mindset. The world often rises to meet the expectations we set for it — whether those expectations are high or low.

In the end, your life is a reflection of your thoughts. **As you think, so are you.** Choose to think better, believe in yourself, and expect more. The mind is powerful—use it to create the life you deserve.

WHEN GROWTH ISN'T A SHARED JOURNEY

You can't carry those who refuse to move.

One of the most challenging life lessons is accepting that not everyone is capable — or willing — to grow. We invest time, energy, and love into people, hoping they'll rise alongside us. But sometimes, no matter how much you want more for someone, they remain stuck in their ways.

You can't want more for people than they want for themselves, especially when they are not complicit.

The Reality of Growth

Growth is a choice. It requires awareness, willingness, and action. Some people embrace change, eager to evolve and discover new possibilities. Others resist it, holding tightly to what's familiar, even if it keeps them stagnant. It's a difficult truth to accept, but **sometimes, a person doesn't have the intellectual ability or emotional capacity to grow.**

This isn't about judgment; it's about recognizing limitations. Not everyone is ready to confront the discomfort that growth demands. For some, leaving behind old habits, mindsets, or environments feels more terrifying than remaining in a cycle of mediocrity.

When you care about someone, wanting to help them rise is natural. You can offer advice, extend opportunities, or pull them forward. But the weight becomes unbearable when your efforts are met with resistance or apathy.

You can't carry someone who refuses to move. It will drain, slow, and eventually hold you back. Carrying the unwilling doesn't lift them higher — it only pulls you lower.

The truth is that **growth is a personal journey.** No matter how much you want to see someone change, you cannot force them to take that path. People must choose growth for themselves, and your efforts will be in vain unless they do.

Knowing When to Move On

The hardest part is knowing when to let go. It's not giving up on them it's accepting reality. You cannot keep pouring into someone who refuses to fill their cup. You cannot wait for someone who refuses to step forward.

Moving on doesn't mean you don't care. It means you value your growth enough to stop holding yourself back. It means recognizing that you deserve to be surrounded by people willing to walk the path with you, not weigh you down.

When you release the need to carry others, you free yourself. You allow yourself to focus on your growth, unburdened by the weight of those unwilling to change. You create space for people who share your hunger for growth, who lift you rather than hold you back.

And in letting go, you offer the greatest gift: the opportunity for them to take responsibility for their journey. Sometimes, people only realize their need to grow when they're left to stand on their own.

A New Path Forward

Not everyone is meant to walk your path. Some will stay behind, and that's okay. It doesn't make them wrong, or you right. It simply means your journeys differ. **You can't carry those who refuse to move.** The best you can do is keep growing, keep pushing forward, and trust that those meant to walk with you will rise to meet you along the way. Ultimately, growth is a choice, and not everyone will make it. But you can. Keep moving. Let go of what holds you back. Your journey is waiting.

THE PURPOSE IN THE PIT

The pit teaches patience, builds resilience, and forces you to confront your fears and doubts, stripping away the falsehoods you once believed about yourself.

Life pushes us into places we never expected to be — dark, lonely, and painful places that feel inescapable. These are the moments that test us, break us, and make us question everything. But what if the very pit you've fallen into was designed for your promotion? What if the depth of your despair is directly connected to the height of your destiny?

Your pit was designed for your promotion. The more bottomless your pit, the greater your elevation.

The Depth of the Pit

It's hard to see anything beyond the darkness when you're in the pit. You feel trapped, abandoned, and overwhelmed. The walls seem too steep to climb, and every attempt to rise feels like slipping further into the abyss.

But what if the pit wasn't a punishment? What if it was preparation? Every struggle, every setback, and every moment of pain shapes you for what lies ahead. The more bottomless the pit, the greater the foundation for what will be built.

Just like a skyscraper needs a deep foundation to reach unimaginable heights, your pit is preparing you for the coming elevation. Without the darkness, you wouldn't appreciate the light. Without the struggle, you wouldn't recognize your strength.

The Purpose of the Pit

It's hard to see the purpose while you're in pain, but every pit holds a lesson. The pit teaches patience, builds resilience, and forces you to confront your fears and doubts, stripping away the falsehoods you once believed about yourself. In the pit, you discover what you're made of.

More importantly, the pit reveals what truly matters. The things you once chased may no longer hold value. The people you relied on may disappear. But in that solitude, you learn to lean on something greater — faith, purpose, and the quiet strength within you.

Always remember that your pit was designed with a purpose. It's not meant to destroy you but to develop you. The trials you're facing aren't obstacles — they're opportunities. They're molding you into the person you're destined to become.

Coming Out of the Pit

You'll emerge from the pit as a different person when the time comes to rise. The same eyes will now see the world differently. The pain that once felt unbearable will become the very thing that propelled you forward. What once seemed like a setback will reveal itself as a setup for something greater.

You'll carry the wisdom gained in the darkness, the strength forged in adversity, and the faith tested and made unbreakable. You'll understand that you wouldn't have the power, perspective, or purpose you now hold without the pit.

Now, you will see things differently after you've come out of the pit. Now, you will see that your pit was for your good.

Rising Higher

The greater the pit, the higher the elevation. Don't despise the struggles. Don't curse the darkness. Embrace the process, even when it feels unbearable. Trust that every tear, every trial, and every lonely moment prepares you for what lies ahead.

Your pit wasn't a mistake — it was a master plan. It was the groundwork for your promotion, the refining fire for your greatness. And when you rise — because you *will* rise —

you'll realize the pit wasn't meant to break you. It was meant to build you.

So, when life pushes you into the depths, remember this: **the deeper the pit, the greater the elevation. Your pit has a purpose. Your rise is coming.**

THE CONDITION OF YOUR HEART: THE KEY TO YOUR OUTCOME

A pure heart doesn't mean a perfect heart it means a heart that releases negativity and embraces compassion, hope, and faith.

The heart is more than just an organ that pumps blood through your veins — it is the seat of your emotions, thoughts, and desires. It holds the essence of who you are, shaping your actions and guiding your path. What resides in your heart will ultimately shape your life because **the condition of your heart will determine your outcome.**

Life has a way of throwing challenges at us — pain, disappointment, betrayal, and loss. Each experience leaves an imprint on the heart. Over time, without care, bitterness can take root, anger can cloud judgment, and resentment can harden even the kindest soul.

That's why it is crucial to guard your heart. **"Keep your heart with all diligence, for out of it spring the issues of life."** What you allow to take residence in your heart will eventually spill over into every aspect of your life. If you harbor unforgiveness, it will show in your relationships. If you nurture fear, it will limit your decisions. If you feed doubt, it will choke your dreams.

The Power of a Pure Heart

A pure heart doesn't mean a perfect heart — it means a heart that releases negativity and embraces compassion, hope, and faith. Your actions follow suit when your heart is aligned with positivity and purpose. You make better choices. You attract better opportunities. You cultivate more profound connections.

A heart filled with love and gratitude creates a life marked by peace and abundance. It allows you to see beyond the pain of the present and recognize the possibilities of the future. It strengthens your resilience, enabling you to rise above adversity and face each day with renewed purpose.

Every thought, every word, every action originates from the heart. Like ripples in a pond, what flows from within you impacts the world around you. A bitter heart breeds conflict, but a compassionate heart fosters unity. A fearful heart builds walls, while a courageous heart opens doors.

Your heart is the compass guiding your life. If the compass is broken, you'll wander. But when your heart is pure, and your intentions are clear, that compass points you toward purpose and fulfillment.

Healing the Heart

If your heart has become heavy with pain or clouded by negativity, take heart — healing is possible. It begins with forgiveness, both for yourself and others. Release the burdens that have weighed you down. Allow grace to soften the rough edges. Nurture your spirit with kindness, understanding, and faith.

Feed your heart with what uplifts you—positive words, loving relationships, meaningful work, and moments of stillness. Protect your peace. Set boundaries. Most importantly, trust that every step you take toward healing strengthens your path toward a better outcome.

A Heart of Purpose

Ultimately, the state of your heart determines the quality of your life. Keep your heart with diligence. Be mindful of what you allow inside because the heart is not just a vessel — it's a guide.

Your life will reflect that light when your heart is filled with love, faith, and purpose. So, guard it, nurture it, and trust it because **the condition of your heart will determine your outcome.** Let it lead you to the life you were meant to live.

THE MIRACLE IN THE BREAKING POINT

There comes a time in life when the weight of the world feels unbearable. The pressure mounts and every step forward feels like a fight for survival. You push and struggle, yet it feels like nothing has changed. Then comes that moment — when your back is against the wall, and you feel like you're about to fall. It's in that very moment, when all seems lost, that the stage is set for something extraordinary. **You are just right for a miracle.**

The Breaking Point

When you're pressed against the wall, the fight-or-flight instinct kicks in. Fear whispers lie: *You're done. There's no way out. You'll never make it.* But what if the wall wasn't the end of your path but the edge of a breakthrough?

Pressure has a way of revealing what you're truly made of. Diamonds are formed under pressure. Gold is refined in fire. And the strongest warriors are forged in the toughest battles. That moment — when you're cornered and out of options — is not where your story ends. It's where your miracle begins.

The Setup for the Supernatural

Think about it: every great story of triumph has a moment when defeat seemed inevitable. The underdog facing impossible odds. The dreamer with nothing left but hope. The person who's lost everything — only to discover they had more strength than they ever realized.

Because miracles aren't born in comfort. They're born in crisis. When your back is against the wall, you're not being buried but planted. What feels like the weight of the world pressing down is the force pushing you to rise.

In the darkest moments, when hope feels distant, the first step toward a miracle is shifting your perspective. Instead of seeing the wall as a dead end, see it as a launching pad. Instead of feeling trapped, recognize that you're in a position to rise.

When you shift your mindset, your actions follow. You stop seeing defeat and start seeing possibility. You stop shrinking and start pushing back. Suddenly, the wall isn't a barrier — it's a sign that you're closer to your breakthrough than ever imagined.

The Power Within

Miracles don't always appear as lightning bolts from the sky. Sometimes, they are the whisper of strength that keeps you going when every part of you wants to give up.

Sometimes, they are finding the courage to take one more step, even when the path is unclear.

When you reach the end of yourself, the impossible happens. Because when your strength runs out, you discover a power greater than yourself. You tap into resilience, faith, and a tenacity you didn't know you had.

You are stronger than you think. The wall isn't there to stop you — it's there to reveal the strength already inside you.

The Miracle Revealed

And then it happens. A door opens. A new opportunity appears. The burden you thought would break you is what made you stronger. The tears that fell watered the seeds of your most tremendous growth. The wall that once held you back becomes the foundation for the life you were always meant to live.

Looking back, you'll see it clearly: the moment you thought your breaking point was actually your breakthrough. The pain that felt unbearable was the pressure that pushed you into purpose. The moment you felt like falling was the moment you learned to fly.

Embrace the Miracle

So, if you're there — if your back is against the wall and you feel like you're about to fall — hold on. The miracle is already in motion. Trust the process. Push through the pressure. Keep believing.

You are just right for a miracle. And when it comes, you'll see that the wall wasn't the end of your story. It was just the beginning.

GOD HAS YOUR RÉSUMÉ

*He's the One who knit you together,
who knows your gifts, your flaws,
and your potential.*

We often scramble to prove ourselves in a world where credentials are everything. We build résumés, collect titles, and chase achievements, hoping the right people will notice our worth. But what if the One who matters most already knows you? What if God has your résumé and knows every detail of who you are — even the parts you try to hide?

The Unseen Qualifications

When we think of résumés, we list our accomplishments: degrees earned, jobs held, awards received. But God's version of your résumé looks a little different. He sees beyond the surface. He knows the moments no one applauded — when you pushed through fear, when you chose kindness over anger, when you forgave even though it hurt. Those unseen victories are the genuine qualifications that shape your character.

While the world judges by external success, God measures the heart. He knows your struggles and celebrates your silent triumphs. When you feel overlooked or underestimated, remember that **God knows you. He sees what others miss.** You may feel like you're waiting for life to start — for the right job, relationship, and opportunity. But God has been preparing you all along. Every experience, whether joyful or painful, has added a line to your résumé. The setbacks that felt like failures were training grounds. The seasons of waiting were shaping your patience. The times of brokenness were strengthening your compassion.

God doesn't waste anything. He uses it all to prepare you for the purpose He's called you to fulfil.

Chosen, Not Forgotten

It's easy to feel forgotten when life doesn't unfold as planned. But God's timing is perfect. Just because your name hasn't been called yet doesn't mean He's overlooked you. He's the One who knit you together, who knows your gifts, your flaws, and your potential.

When the time is right, God will open doors no man can shut. He will place you in rooms you never expected to enter. And when He calls your name, it won't be because of who you know or what you've done — it will be because He knows you.

Trust the Process

So, when doubt creeps in when you wonder if you're enough, remember this: **God has your résumé.** He knows your every strength and weakness, your every triumph and tear. Trust that He guides your path, even when the road is unclear.

You don't have to prove yourself to Him. You don't need to embellish your story or strive for perfection. God's already seen the work you've put in. He knows the weight you've carried. And in His eyes, you are more than qualified for the purpose He has for you.

Take heart. Your time is coming. Trust that the One who holds your résumé holds your future, too.

THE POWER OF VERSATILITY

Versatility doesn't mean being perfect at everything. It means being open, adaptable, and willing to learn.

Versatility is a gift. It's the ability to adapt confidently and gracefully and grow into different roles. In a constantly changing world, versatility isn't just valuable — it's essential. Those willing to stretch themselves, learn new skills, and embrace different experiences often find doors open where others only see walls.

One-dimensional people limit themselves to a single path. They may excel in one area, but when life demands flexibility, they struggle. However, those who cultivate versatility can navigate life's unexpected twists with resilience and purpose. Being multi-faceted means you're not confined to just one way of thinking, skill set, or vision of your life. It means you're open to being used in ways you may never have imagined.

Think about the most outstanding leaders, innovators, and change-makers throughout history. They weren't just good at one thing — they dared to explore, adapt, and grow. They understood that every skill, experience, and challenge prepared them for something greater. They didn't resist change — they embraced it. And in doing so, they unlocked opportunities that others missed.

God can do amazing things through people who are willing to be stretched. When you allow yourself to become multi-faceted, you give Him more to work with. One moment, He may call you to lead. The next, He may need you to serve. One day, you may be a teacher, and the next, a student. Your willingness to grow in different areas makes you a vessel ready for any assignment.

Versatility doesn't mean being perfect at everything. It means being open, adaptable, and willing to learn. It means embracing the unknown with faith and trusting that every experience — even the uncomfortable ones — shapes you for a greater purpose. It means recognizing that every skill you develop is another tool in your toolbox, another way to make an impact, and another avenue for God to use you.

So, don't confine yourself to a single lane. Dare to explore your potential. Learn new things. Step outside your comfort zone. Be willing to serve in ways you've never considered before. The more versatile you become; the more opportunities will come your way — not just from the world but from God Himself.

Because when you're multi-faceted, you're not just prepared for one role. You're ready for whatever purpose God places in your path.

THE WEIGHT OF LEADERSHIP

It means having the courage to admit when you're wrong and the humility to listen to those who may know more than you.

Leadership is not a title — it is a responsibility. When people trust you to lead them, they place their hopes, efforts, and often their futures in your hands. That kind of trust is sacred and should never be taken lightly. True leaders understand their role is not about power or recognition but about serving those who have chosen to follow them. To fail them is to break that trust.

Every leader stands at the intersection of vision and responsibility. It's easy to cast a vision, to inspire people with words and promises, but the accurate measure of leadership is found in action. People don't follow because of what you say — they follow because of what you *do*. When you're at the helm, every decision you make sends ripples through the lives of those who trust you to guide them. That weight isn't a burden; it's a privilege.

The danger comes when leaders forget who they're serving. Some become consumed by ambition, using their position for personal gain while neglecting the people who helped them rise. Others buckle under pressure, retreating into indecision or apathy when the weight becomes too heavy. But true leaders understand that leadership is not about comfort; it's about sacrifice. It's about showing up — even when you're tired or uncertain — because others are counting on you.

A leader's success is measured not by personal achievement but by the growth and well-being of those they lead. Are you empowering others? Are you creating space for people to thrive? Are you making decisions with integrity, knowing that your choices impact more than just yourself? Leadership means putting others before yourself. It means having the courage to admit when you're wrong and the humility to listen to those who may know more than you. It means staying steady in the storm and being a source of strength when others feel weak.

A leader's greatest failure is forgetting the hearts behind the work. Every organization, team, and family is made up of people—people with dreams, fears, and stories. Leadership is not about steering a ship but caring for the souls on board. If you lose sight of that, you've already failed.

Leaders must not fail those who let them lead because leadership is never about the leader — it's about the people. The most outstanding leaders are not remembered for the heights they reached but for the hands they held along the way. If you've been given the gift of leadership, honor it. Rise to the responsibility. Show up daily, not for yourself, but for those who trust you to guide them.

They are watching. They are believing in you. Don't let them down.

FAILURE BEGINS IN THE MIND

Failure is a feeling long before it becomes a reality.

Failure is not just an event — it's a mindset. Before it becomes a reality, failure takes root as a feeling, whispering doubts into your heart and clouding your vision. Most battles are won or lost in the mind before they ever play out in real life. What you believe about yourself shapes your actions, and your actions shape your outcomes.

Have you ever faced a challenge and, before even trying, thought to yourself, *I'm not good enough, I'll probably mess this up*, or *There's no way I can succeed*? That quiet voice of doubt may seem harmless at first, but the more you listen to it, the louder it becomes. It convinces you to shrink back, play it safe, and avoid taking risks. And slowly, you start living out your feared failure without realising it.

But where does that feeling come from? Sometimes, it's past experiences — when you stumbled or someone told you that you weren't capable. Other times, it's the fear of judgment, not measuring up, or the pressure of expectations weighing heavily on your shoulders. Whatever the source, the result is the same: doubt creeps in and plants a seed of failure long before any real setback occurs.

The danger lies in allowing those feelings to shape your reality. When you believe failure is inevitable, you stop trying. You hesitate when you should move forward. You give half-effort, expecting things to fall apart, and in doing so, you unknowingly pave the way for the outcome you feared.

But what if you could change the narrative? What if you could recognize those feelings for what they are — *just feelings* — and refuse to let them control your actions? The most successful people in the world aren't the ones who never felt doubt. They're the ones who pushed forward despite it. They understood that the feeling of failure is just a moment of vulnerability, not a prophecy of defeat.

Failure only becomes real when you accept it. Until then, every setback is just a lesson, every delay is just a moment of preparation, and every challenge is an opportunity to grow stronger. You are not defined by the moments when doubt whispers in your ear — your response defines you.

So, the next time failure tries to make itself at home in your mind, remember this: You have a choice. You can let that feeling control you or rise above it. The path to success isn't about never feeling doubt; it's about refusing to let that doubt make your decisions.

Failure is a feeling long before it becomes a reality but only if you let it.

THE PRICELESS REWARDS OF INTEGRITY AND AUTHENTICITY

When you live authentically, you attract genuine relationships and opportunities that align with your true self.

Integrity and authenticity cost nothing financially, yet they are among the most valuable traits a person can possess. In a world where people often chase status, wealth, and approval, standing firmly in your truth is a rare and powerful act. It may not require a financial investment, but the rewards it brings to your life and your journey are immeasurable.

The Foundation of Integrity

Integrity is the unwavering commitment to doing what is right, even when no one is watching. It's about being honest in your actions, keeping your promises, and aligning your values with your behaviour. Integrity isn't a performance for others — it's a covenant you make with yourself. When you operate with integrity, you build a life of trust and respect. People come to know that your word holds weight and that your actions are dependable.

But integrity isn't always straightforward. It may mean standing alone when the crowd is taking an easier path. It may mean turning down opportunities that compromise your values. At times, the cost feels high — but what you gain is far greater. You gain peace of mind, a clear conscience, and the ability to look at yourself in the mirror without regret. That is a wealth no amount of money can buy.

Authenticity goes hand in hand with integrity. It means showing up as your true self without masks or pretenses. In a world that often rewards conformity, being authentic can feel risky. It takes courage to embrace who you are and live in alignment with your values, even when others don't understand or approve.

Yet, authenticity is magnetic. When you live authentically, you attract genuine relationships and opportunities that align with your true self. People are drawn to those who are genuine, who aren't afraid to be vulnerable, and who speak their truth with kindness and conviction. Living authentically frees you from the exhausting need to pretend. It allows you to walk through life easily, knowing that you are accepted for who you indeed are — not for who you're trying to be.

The Deep Rewards

The rewards of integrity and authenticity cannot be measured in dollars, but they enrich your life profoundly. They grant you inner peace, knowing that your actions are aligned with your beliefs. They build lasting trust with those around you, creating relationships rooted in respect and honesty. They open doors to meaningful opportunities because the right doors open when you stand in your truth.

Most importantly, integrity and authenticity deepen your spiritual and personal growth. They keep you grounded in what matters most and remind you that success isn't defined by external validation but by the quiet confidence of knowing you are walking the right path.

In the end, money may come and go, but the wealth of a life with integrity and authenticity is eternal. So, stand firm in your values, speak your truth, and live in a way that honors who you are. The cost is nothing, but the rewards are everything.

THE ART OF LISTENING — THE SECRET TO GREAT SPEAKING

*Listen to understand, not to reply.
Listen with curiosity and compassion.
Practice patience. Pay attention to
the world around you, and let what
you hear shape your words.*

When we think of great speakers, we often picture powerful voices commanding attention, eloquent words flowing effortlessly, and captivating stories that stir hearts and minds. But what sets the genuinely remarkable speakers apart is not just their ability to speak — it's their ability to listen.

Listening is the foundation of meaningful communication. Words without understanding are just noise. A speaker who doesn't listen is like a musician playing without hearing the other instruments — out of sync, disconnected, and ultimately forgettable. But a speaker who listens deeply becomes attuned to the room's rhythm, the people's hearts, and the moment's pulse. This creates not just a speech but a connection.

Listening teaches you what matters most. Every great speech begins with understanding your audience. What do they care about? What are their fears, hopes, and dreams? When you take the time to listen — whether through conversations, reading the room, or paying attention to the world around you — you gather the threads of meaning that weave into a message people genuinely need to hear.

Great listeners also pick up on unspoken cues. Body language, tone, and energy reveal just as much as words. When you're present and attentive, you can sense when your message is landing and when you need to shift. It allows you to respond, adapt, and meet people where they are.

Listening Builds Trust

A speaker who listens is a speaker who cares. People don't just want to be talked *at* — they want to be *heard*. When you take the time to listen, you show respect. You build trust. And when people feel heard, they're more willing to listen to your words.

In conversations, this means asking questions and allowing space for answers. On stage, it means observing reactions and making room for silence. In life, it means valuing other voices as much as your own. The more you listen, the more your words carry weight.

Listening Sharpens Your Message

Listening refines your words. It helps you understand what you want to say and what people need to hear. It teaches you to strip away the unnecessary, speak with clarity, and deliver resonant messages. When you listen, you learn the language of your audience — the metaphors that move them, the stories that stick, the emotions that drive action.

Some of the greatest speeches in history weren't born from a desire to be heard but from a desire to serve. Martin Luther King Jr. listened to the cries for justice before he ever dreamed of giving a speech. Nelson Mandela listened to the voices of his people before he ever spoke of freedom. Their words changed the world because they arose from a heart that understood.

The Art of the Pause

One of the most potent tools a speaker can use is silence. Pausing gives your audience time to reflect, but it also gives *you* time to listen — not just to the room but to yourself. It's in those quiet moments that you connect most deeply. You hear the heartbeat of the message. You feel the weight of the moment.

Becoming a Listener First

To become a great speaker, start by becoming a great listener. Listen to understand, not to reply. Listen with curiosity and compassion. Practice patience. Pay attention to the world around you, and let what you hear shape your words.

The greatest speakers aren't those who demand the most attention but those who offer the deepest understanding. The art of speaking begins with the art of listening. When you master that, your words will no longer just be heard — they will be *felt.*

THE ETERNAL STUDENT — STAYING RELEVANT AS A TEACHER

A teacher who stops learning stops teaching — but a teacher who remains a student will never be forgotten.

A teacher's greatest strength isn't just what they know—it's their willingness to keep learning. The moment a teacher ceases to be a student; they begin to drift into irrelevance. Teaching is not about reaching a destination of knowledge but about embracing a growth journey. The world is ever-changing, and those who refuse to adapt risk being left behind, not just in knowledge but in connection with those they aim to teach.

The Danger of Stagnation

Knowledge is not static. New ideas emerge, old theories evolve, and technology reshapes the learning landscape daily. A teacher who believes they've "arrived" — who stops questioning, exploring, and expanding their understanding — slowly loses touch with the very essence of what it means to educate. They become rigid, holding onto outdated methods while the world moves forward without them.

More dangerously, they lose connection with their students. Each new generation brings different perspectives, challenges, and ways of thinking. To remain relevant, teachers must learn new information and new ways to communicate, motivate, and inspire. When a teacher stops learning, their words may still be heard but stop resonating.

Being a lifelong student requires humility. It means admitting you don't know everything and realizing that's a good thing. The best teachers understand that learning is reciprocal and recognize that their students have lessons to teach. Every classroom is a space for shared discovery, where knowledge flows in multiple directions.

Questions or challenges don't threaten a teacher who remains a student—they energize them. They view curiosity as a spark for growth and embrace the unknown with excitement rather than fear. This humility fosters an environment where students feel empowered to explore and engage, knowing their teacher is on the journey with them.

Adapting to Change

The world is evolving faster than ever before. Technology, culture, and global perspectives are shifting, reshaping how we communicate and understand each other.

A teacher who stops learning becomes anchored to the past, unable to equip students for the future.

Great teachers adapt. They seek new methods, experiment with fresh ideas, and aren't afraid to innovate. Whether mastering new technology, exploring diverse perspectives, or embracing unconventional teaching methods, the willingness to evolve keeps a teacher impactful.

Remaining a student isn't a burden, It's a gift. Lifelong learners experience the thrill of discovery over and over again. They stay curious, energized, and passionate about their craft. This passion is contagious, inspiring students to absorb knowledge and seek it themselves.

A teacher who continues to learn leads by example. They show their students that growth is never finished, that curiosity is a lifelong companion, and that wisdom is not in having all the answers but in never stopping the search.

A Legacy of Growth

In the end, the most incredible legacy a teacher can leave is not a body of knowledge but a mindset of growth. Students may forget facts, but they will always remember the teacher who ignited their curiosity, who showed them that learning is a lifelong pursuit, and who embodied the very principles they taught.

A teacher who stops learning stops teaching, but a teacher who remains a student will never be forgotten. Stay curious, stay humble, stay relevant. The world needs more eternal students.

Made in the USA
Las Vegas, NV
25 April 2025